MINNESOTA-ONTARIO
IRON ORE RAILROADS

MINNESOTA-ONTARIO IRON ORE RAILROADS

PATRICK C. DORIN

© Copyright 2002 TLC Publishing, Inc.

1387 Winding Creek Lane
Lynchburg, VA 24503-3776

All Rights Reserved. No part of this work may be reproduced without the written permission of the copyright holder, except for brief quotations used in reviews or other "fair use."

International Standard Book Number   1-883089-73-5
Library of Congress Control Number   2002101474

Design and Production by
Kevin J. Holland
type&DESIGN
Burlington, Ontario

Produced on the MacOS™

Printed by
Walsworth Publishing Company
Marceline, Missouri 64658

Front cover—
A southbound Duluth, Missabe & Iron Range ore train passes Wyman en route to Two Harbors, Minnesota, on October 4, 1997. Wyman is 47.3 miles from Two Harbors on the DM&IR's Iron Range Division. DAVID C. SCHAUER

Title page—
Five perfectly matched Erie Mining Company F-units in an A-B-B-B-A combination arrive at Taconite Harbor, Minnesota, with an ore train in this late-1950s scene. BASGEN PHOTOGRAPHY, DAN MACKEY COLLECTION

Other books by Patrick C. Dorin from TLC Publishing, Inc.—

Western Pacific Locomotives and Equipment
Louisville & Nashville—The Old Reliable (with Charles Castner and Ron Flanary)
Louisville & Nashville Passenger Trains—The Pan American Era 1921–1971 (with Charles Castner and Robert Chapman)
Chicago & North Western Passenger Service—The Postwar Years
Chicago & North Western Passenger Equipment
The Challenger
Missouri Pacific Freight Trains and Equipment
Missouri Pacific Passenger Service—The Postwar Years
Michigan-Ontario Iron Ore Railroads

Dedicated to

Tim Schandel
Tom Gannon
Claudia Busch
Ron Kaziukewicz

and the staff of the

LAKE SUPERIOR RAILROAD MUSEUM

and to

Robert Blomquist
Jim Morin
David R. Carlson
Dan Mackey
Tom Dorin

and the many other members of the

LAKE SUPERIOR TRANSPORTATION CLUB

Who have created an incredible organization for history, education, research,
and many opportunities to ride a wide variety of passenger trains
from Duluth-Superior and elsewhere in Minnesota, Wisconsin, and Ontario during the past 30 years.

ACKNOWLEDGMENTS

No book would ever be possible without the assistance and wisdom of many people. I would like to thank the following people for their time, efforts, photographs, advice, proofreading, and extensive research for this book.

Thomas W. Dixon, Jr. of TLC Publishing conceived and encouraged the format of this book, and Kevin J. Holland performed the design and layout work. My wife Karen spent hours proofreading and on the road for research and photography work.

David C. Schauer of the Missabe Historical Society provided many insights with his review of the text and photographs for the Duluth, Missabe & Iron Range Railway. Robert Blomquist compiled rosters of the DM&IR, Burlington Northern, and the Burlington Northern Santa Fe ore car fleets and provided a wide selection of photographs. John C. Luecke provided assistance with a variety of maps.

David R. Carlson, Kurt Johnson, Tina Wester, J. Michael McCoshen, Patrick Hiatte, Fred Rutt, Michael Weston, Susan Carlson, and many others provided assistance with the BN and BNSF chapter.

John Holm and Cory Wills of the Northshore Mining Company reviewed the text and provided additional information regarding rosters and other details of their operation.

David Oviatt, Tom Sample, and Martin Fair assisted with rosters and other information regarding operations on the DM&IR during the last two decades of the 20th century. Tim Schandel of the Lake Superior Railroad Museum and Douglas Buell, formerly of LTV Steel Mining, also provided valuable assistance, and Kevin Acker drew several of the ore lines maps.

The following people were kind enough to share their photography—and some even went out and took additional photographs of key elements of the ore lines: Thomas Dorin, Michael Dorin, Robert C. Anderson, Michael Burlaga, Tom Carlson, Edward L. Kanak, William S. Kuba, Jeff Lemke, Jim Morin, Fred Headon, Bryan Martyniuk, Steven Ruce, Tim Schandel, and Stafford Swain.

To all of you, a huge "thank you" in a thousand different ways. Should an acknowledgment have been inadvertently missed here, please accept my apology and trust that it will be found in the appropriate place within the text. Again, a SOO-per thank you to all.

INTRODUCTION

Minnesota-Ontario Iron Ore Railroads covers the wide variety of ore-hauling railroads in northeastern Minnesota and northwestern Ontario. These railroads fed iron ore through six sets of dock facilities from Duluth-Superior to Thunder Bay, Ontario.

The largest operations included the Duluth, Missabe & Iron Range Railway and the Great Northern Railway. The original Reserve Mining Company ranked third in terms of tonnage handled from their mine to the Silver Bay plant.

This book looks at train operations for moving the Minnesota-Ontario ore from the mines to the docks, and also reviews the all-rail ore operations during the last two decades of the 20th century. In many cases, the Michigan ore lines participated in the all-rail movements from the Duluth-Superior area to the steel producing centers.

Each specific railroad chapter includes descriptions of the train, yard, and dock operations as well as the ore car equipment owned by each company. The objective of the photo coverage is to illustrate the types of trains each railroad operated as well as the rolling stock, motive power, and the ore dock systems. Motive power rosters are included for the regional railroad and mining companies dedicated to ore haulage.

We have lost some of the original railroads to mergers, such as the Northern Pacific and the Great Northern, which became key parts of Burlington Northern and, later, Burlington Northern Santa Fe. Some of the railroads are completely out of the ore business now, such as the Soo Line, Canadian National, and the original Erie Mining Company, known in its last years as LTV.

This leaves but three rail routes in Northern Minnesota: the DM&IR, BNSF, and Northshore Mining, as compared to seven companies during the 1960s: the DM&IR, GN, NP, SOO, CN, Erie Mining, and Reserve Mining.

We could, and should, actually count eight railroads—the Chicago Great Western served the Spring Valley ore region in far southeastern Minnesota. Ore was loaded into CGW 50- and 70-ton coal hoppers and shipped all-rail to the Chicago are—interchanging with the Elgin, Joliet & Eastern Railway.

The companion volume to this book, *Michigan-Ontario Iron Ore Railroads*, describes the train operations from Ashland, Wisconsin, through to the the ports on Lake Huron and Georgian Bay.

I hope that readers will find these books useful not only for their presentation of the operation's history and ore handling operations, but also as an aid to modelers choosing to duplicate in miniature these railroad systems that handled the world's heaviest trains.

Happy Railroading,

Patrick C. Dorin
Superior, Wisconsin
July 1, 2002

CONTENTS

CHAPTER 1 THE DULUTH, MISSABE & IRON RANGE RAILWAY | 2

CHAPTER 2 THE GREAT NORTHERN RAILWAY | 36
THE NORTHERN PACIFIC RAILWAY
THE BURLINGTON NORTHERN RAILROAD
THE BURLINGTON NORTHERN SANTA FE RAILROAD

CHAPTER 3 NORTHSHORE MINING / CYPRUS NORTH SHORE / RESERVE MINING | 64

CHAPTER 4 LTV / ERIE MINING | 80

CHAPTER 5 THE SOO LINE RAILROAD | 92

CHAPTER 6 CANADIAN NATIONAL RAILWAYS | 98

Erie Mining became LTV Steel Mining Co. in 1986, but the railroad's venerable F-units kept rolling. Here, LTV F9 No. 4211 is leading an eastbound train approaching Taconite Harbor on July 18, 1998. DAVID C. SCHAUER

1 THE DULUTH, MISSA

ABOVE: After doing without switch engines since the 1970s or before, the DM&IR purchased an NW2 from the Elgin, Joliet & Eastern and assigned it No. 11. The switcher works the Proctor, Minnesota, roundhouse area and retains part of its EJ&E color scheme in this July 1998 photo. DAVID C. SCHAUER

FACING PAGE: This view shows the DM&IR's Two Harbors, Minnesota, docks No. 1 and 2 prior to modification with conveyor belt systems for handling taconite pellets to the No. 2 dock. Note the size of the 1000-foot ore vessel alongside dock No. 1. It is easy to see why the 1000-footers would have to change sides or move from one dock to the other to create an evenly distributed load when using only the regular gravity chutes for loading. BASGEN PHOTOGRAPHY, DAN MACKEY COLLECTION

The "Missabe," as the DM&IR is ofter called, is the most prominent iron ore hauler in the Lake Superior region. It is still No. 1 in terms of tonnage handled annually and, as of 2002, still served more mines and pelletizing plants than any other ore line in the Lake Superior region.

The DM&IR has changed dramatically over the past 30 years. The type and configuration of the ore trains has changed from the uniformity of SD9s and SD18s hauling 24-foot ore cars and a caboose, to a wide assortment of motive power from several railroads pulling 100-ton-capacity coal hoppers in ore service with a computer on the rear end!

On the other hand, DM&IR ore trains still consist of the 24-foot ore cars, some of which have been rebuilt. So it can be said

IRON RANGE RAILROAD

This map shows the extent of the DM&IR system during the 1950s. Note the double-track lines from Duluth and Two Harbors. DM&IR

A northbound empty train rolls along the now single-track portion of the Missabe Division near Alborn on August 19, 1995. This particular train consists of regular ore cars without extensions and is headed for the EVTAC plant. Note the space adjacent to the track, which at one time was the second main line for the Missabe Division.
DAVID C. SCHAUER

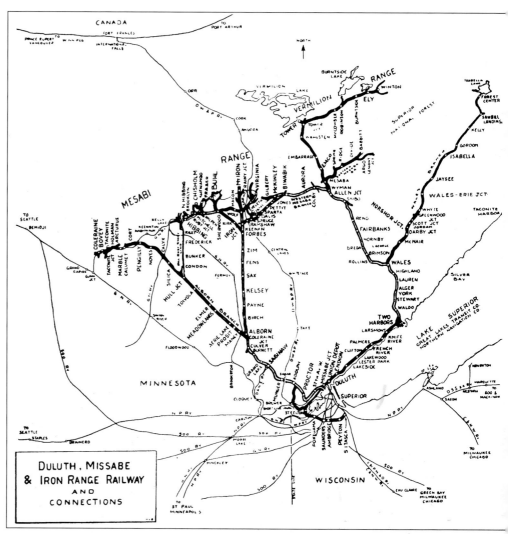

An ore train load of pellets departs the EVTAC plant (Eveleth Taconite) for the Proctor Yard with the 400 in the lead on August 8, 1998. Known as "400 South" to the dispatcher, the train will travel over the Missabe Division to Proctor.

The "400 South" consisted of 146 loads in regular ore cars. BOTH, PATRICK C. DORIN

said that the DM&IR has changed—and it has not changed. The key to this statement is the marketing program provided by the company and the service operating requirements of the different shippers and consignees.

The DM&IR story would really take an entire book, and we have much to be thankful to Frank King for his publications on the company. The Missabe Railroad Historical Society also deserves a substantial amount of credit for the work its members have done in preserving the railroad's history as well as technical information for model railroaders.

ROAD OPERATIONS TO DULUTH AND TWO HARBORS

The road operations are relatively simple to describe with but a few differences between the 1950s and 2000s. The road ore trains are called at the Proctor or Two Harbors yards, sent north for natural ore or pellets, usually loading at a pelletizing plant, and return to the respective yard. Train lengths may range from about 110 to 120 cars out of Two Harbors, and anywhere from 130 to 180 out of Proctor. Train lengths are determined by the loading specifications at the mine and/or plant. However, there can be some dramatic differences. Train lengths have been as short as 50 cars and as long as 236.

The road operations are divided into two divisions: the MISSABE, Duluth to the Range, and the IRON RANGE, Two Harbors to the Range. Missabe Division trains are the longest and heaviest with fewer hills and other geographical obstacles. Missabe Division crews run thru from Proctor to the mining company facility and return. Iron Range Division crews also run from Two Harbors directly to a pellet plant and return. Although at one time, Biwabik was a crew change point for the Two Harbors crews.

The road crews are also responsible for weighing the trains upon the return to Proctor or Two Harbors. The Missabe Division scale is

Number 216 North has a train load of limestone and is headed for the Minntac Plant on September 3, 1995. The train is near Zim, Minnesota, on the Missabe Division. DAVID C. SCHAUER

On August 8, 1998, No. 202 North was approaching Wolf in CTC territory on the Missabe Division en route to the Minntac Plant.

The Minntac train consists of the mini-quad rebuilt ore cars with side extensions. Note the repainting of the reporting marks over the insignia. BOTH, PATRICK C. DORIN

located just north of the Proctor Yard. Depending upon the size of the train, the crew may weigh the entire train or just half of it. If the latter is the case, a Proctor yard crew will complete the weighing process.

The Iron Range Division scale is located a Highland, about 15 miles north of the Two Harbors yard. The road crew weighs the entire train as it begins its descent down the hill to Lake Superior. Once the trains are weighed, they are then spotted on one of the receiving yard tracks.

Road operations on the Missabe Division have taken on a new responsibility for the mining companies. Beginning in the late 1980s, the steel companies have been shipping limestone to the port of Duluth for movement to the pelletizing plants for the manufacture of fluxed pellets. This eliminates the need for mixing the pellets with limestone at the steel mill. A fluxed pellet is a far more effective product for making certain kinds of steel which must be of a consistent quality. Since the pellets have a consistent percentage of limestone, the steel quality levels can be maintained with an easier process.

Consequently, certain northbound trains from Duluth and Proctor transport limestone. The limestone is delivered to the pelletizing plant where it is unloaded and stored until used in the pellet manufacturing process. During the shipping season, the limestone is handled in the mini-quad ore cars to Minorca, while the Minntac plant is served by side-dump cars. Winter season trains have consisted of not only DM&IR and former Minntac side-dump cars, but also cars from the Union Pacific, Missouri Pacific, Canadian National and other railroads.

The Missabe Division road operations serve three mines and pelletizing plants: the Minntac EVTAC and Minorca. The Iron Range trains

Limestone is also handled in regular ore cars as illustrated by this northbound train passing the junction switch for the Interstate Branch at Adolph on the Missabe Division. The engineer has the 302 North in the eighth notch and the train is picking up speed. PATRICK C. DORIN

Switching over to the Iron Range Division, four diesel units are handling a trainload of natural ore from the Auburn Mine en route to Two Harbors. The train is southbound near Gilbert, Minnesota, on April 26, 1997. DAVID C. SCHAUER

FACING PAGE, TOP: December 23, 1995, saw this southbound train from Minntac heading for Two Harbors passing Skibo, Minnesota.

FACING PAGE, BOTTOM: The DM&IR operates a freight train over both the Iron Range and Missabe Division main lines, via Proctor to the "Range" and Two Harbors, returning the next day. Designated "MRF" (Miscellaneous Road Freight), it is shown at Skibo on July 7, 1997.

LEFT: Southbound ore trains are weighed in motion at Highland, 14 miles north of Two Harbors. This is one of the few stretches of double track on the Iron Range Division.

BELOW: A southbound loaded train passes Wyman en route to Two Harbors on October 4, 1997. ALL, DAVID C. SCHAUER

erve both the Minntac and the Minorca Plant as well as the Auburn Mine. The Auburn Mine is he only natural ore producer at the time of this vriting. This ore has been shipped through Two Harbors for boat loading or to Superior, Wisconsin for a connection with the Wisconsin Central for all-rail movements to the USX steel mill in Gary, Indiana.

The Minorca Plant is located north of Virginia, Minnesota on the Duluth, Winnipeg &

Upon arrival at Two Harbors the road crew's work is complete. This train rounds the curve and glides slowly into the ore yard on July 4, 1998. The next job will belong to the switch crews for dumping the cars on either the dock or the dumper for ground strorage.
DAVID C. SCHAUER

As can be seen in a comparison with the map on page 4, the railroad has been trimmed substantially since the 1970s. In addition, the line from Proctor to Fairlane is now single track, and the route from Duluth to Two Harbors is now part of the County Transportation Systems and the North Shore Scenic Railroad. DM&IR

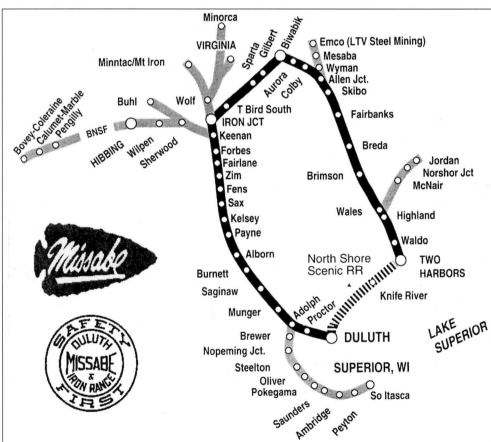

Pacific Railway. Consequently, the DM&IR trains operate over the DW&P from a point south of Virginia to the Minorca Plant.

As a side note, the DW&P also serves the EVTAC plant through the delivery of bentonite clay for the pellet production at that location Originally, there was a proposal that the Evelet plant was to be served on a pool basis with th DW&P, DM&IR and the Soo Line. Howeve these plans were shelved in the early 1960s whe

Passenger specials frequently operate over the DM&IR, especially during the summer and fall months. This July 22, 1998, two-car special consists of the company's business combine and business car, the *Northland*. DAVID C. SCHAUER

The North Shore Scenic Railroad operates an RDC-1 passenger coach between Duluth and Two Harbors for summer tourist rides along the North Shore, as here on August 7, 1998. The trains arrive and depart Two Harbors depot and operate over the DM&IR within the Two Harbors Terminal area. Between Duluth and a point just south of Two Harbors, the NSSR operates over the former DM&IR trackage, which now belongs to St. Louis and Lake Counties. The DM&IR once operated its own RDC-3 between Duluth, Two Harbors, and Ely, Minnesota, over this trackage. PATRICK C. DORIN

The *Mining Engineer's Special* requires more equipment, and subsequently, these special passenger trains included cars from the Lake Superior Railroad Museum, and even the former Wisconsin Central Railroad. On September 13, 1997, the six-car train included two cars each from the LSRM and the WC. Photographed at Wilpen on the Iron Range Division. DAVID C. SCHAUER

11

it was realized that the DM&IR would be the most effective hauler. The DW&P did not have access to ore dock facilities, although part of the idea considered the use of Soo Line ore cars with the Soo doing the switching and dumping the ore on the NP dock in Superior. (During World-War II, the DW&P interchanged Canadian Steep Rock ore with the Great Northern Railway in Superior for shipment over the Allouez docks.)

Train density on the Missabe Division ranges from three to six trains in each direction daily. The Iron Range Division ranges from four to six round trips per day. A local freight train, the MRF (Miscellaneous Road Freight) operates over both divisions twice a week from Proctor to the Range to Two Harbors returning on the following day.

MESABI RANGE OPERATIONS

During the 1960s, the DM&IR's Mesabi Range operations consisted of mine run operations (spotting empties and picking up loads at the various mines), local freight train services across the range from Biwabik to Coleraine, and what were known as "ping-pong" operations. The latter train services provided an interchange of ore loads between the two divisions for shipment to either the Duluth or Two Harbors docks. Consequently, one could find both empties and loads moving in the same directions.

Since the early 1980s, the lines to Coleraine have been abandoned, both from the Missabe Division main line near Alborn and west from the Hibbing Area. The DM&IR does have trackage rights over the BN (now BNSF) to Coleraine

The Evtac Plant. Note the raw ore going through the dumper with the empty cars to the right. On the other hand, the silo loading facility is loading outbound pellets.
BASGEN PHOTOGRAPHY,
DAN MACKEY COLLECTION

The Minntac Plant while under construction. BASGEN PHOTOGRAPHY, DAN MACKEY COLLECTION

The DM&IR would never really be called a "coal hauler," but it is! A four-unit Keenan Switch job headed by No. 206 is coupling up to a block of coal loads to be delivered to the power plant at Colby on August 8, 1996. Colby is about 50 miles from Two Harbors on the Iron Range Division. PATRICK C. DORIN

but is currently used for commercial freight service only. The line to Ely is also gone. Ely was once the northern terminal of the Iron Range Division that now ends at Hoyt Lakes, the site of the LTV Steel Mining Company pellet plant. With the shrinkage of the routes on both the Mesabi and Vermilion Iron Ranges, there is no longer any need for the "ping-pong" crews. Local freight services are handled out of Keenan Yard for clay and other materials being delivered to the taconite plants, and also for coal deliveries to a power plant in Hoyt Lakes. The Laskin plant coal traffic is received from the BNSF, which in turn is delivered in sections to the power plant

One very busy piece of trackage on the Missabe Division is the segment between the EVTAC Plant and the Thunder Bird Mine. The assignments for handling the raw ore from the mine to the plant are known as "T-Birds." The 9:00 a.m. T-Bird is taking on its first load of raw ore for the day on August 8, 1998. PATRICK C. DORIN

Another view of the loading facility at the T-Bird Mine. PATRICK C. DORIN

Coal empties continue to move south along the Missabe Division main line as the trains must back into Keenan Yard. PATRICK C. DORIN

near Hoyt Lakes. (At one time, coal was delivered by Great Lakes ships for transloading into DM&IR ore cars for delivery to power companies.)

Mine run services (since the opening of the EVTAC Plant in 1965) are operated between the EVTAC Fairlane Plant and the open pit Thunder Bird mine north of Iron Junction. These trains consist of 86 ore cars equipped with 20 inch extensions. The extensions are grooved for the car dumpers at the EVTAC plant. Crews operate around the clock between the mine and the plant. These trains were once also equipped with bay-window cabooses.

The T-Bird loads approaching Fairlane and the EVTAC Plant. PATRICK C. DORIN

A coal train's back-up move into Keenan Yard is now almost completed as the train has cleared the main line of the Missabe Division. PATRICK C. DORIN

The center for all operations on the Mesabi Range is Keenan. This yard provides storage for empties designated for loading at various points, and the classification work for loads going to various destinations. The yard also stores and repairs ore cars as well as serving as a motive power facility.

ORE DOCK AND YARD OPERATIONS

The Duluth, Missabe & Iron Range is the only railroad now operating *two* ore shipping ports. Both facilities—at Two Harbors and Duluth—consist of pellet ground storage areas and pocket-type ore docks equipped with both chutes and

The Duluth docks after completion of the taconite storage area. Trains dump the pellets on the dock, which are then transported to the stock piles by conveyor belts and the stacker. For boat loading, a reclaimer scoops up the pellets to be returned to the ore dock via conveyor. Three boats were loading at the DM&IR docks when the photo was taken. These are the largest Great Lakes docks. BASGEN PHOTOGRAPHY, DAN MACKEY COLLECTION

U. S. Steel's *Roger Blough* loads taconite pellets at the Duluth dock. The conveyor system is on top of the dock. Note the rebuilt ore cars in the foreground. PATRICK C. DORIN

conveyor loading systems for the super ore lake carriers.

The Two Harbors facility unloads ore cars either through a car dumper in the yard, or on top of the ore docks for dock storage or direct load into a ship.

The Duluth dock system unloads the ore cars on top of dock No. 6, and moves the pellets to the ground storage area by a conveyor system. When the pellets are called for a boat load, they move back to the dock by the conveyor system and placed on still another conveyor system that sits on one of the railroad tracks. This moveable conveyor system loads the pockets on the west side of the ore dock for boat loading.

When trains arrive in Two Harbors, they are inspected and switched for either unloading

The Duluth dock is now not only equipped with the conveyor chutes for loading the wide 1000-foot vessels, but it can also handle inbound limestone for the taconite plants. The *Philip R. Clarke*, a self-unloader, is pouring limestone into the intake system, which in turn transports the limestone for stockpile storage to the left of the ore dock. Note the standard chutes to the right of the photo. PATRICK C. DORIN

In order to accommodate the larger 1000-foot ore carriers, the DM&IR modified the loading area of the No. 6 ore dock with longer spouts equipped with conveyor belts. With this modification, ships such as the *Columbia Star* could simply stay in one place as the conveyor belt chute system can easily place an even and balanced load onboard the ship. BASGEN PHOTOGRAPHY, DAN MACKEY COLLECTION

Inbound pellets are dumped on the ore dock on the left side. The pellets then travel by belt to storage areas for a specific taconite plant as well as the specific pellet product (fluxed for plain).

through the car dumper, or for movement on to the top of the dock. A yard crew handles the placement of ore cars for either the dumper or the ore dock. Once the cars are emptied, they are again inspected and assembled for an empty train back to the Mesabi Range, most often the Minntac plant.

When the trains arrive in Proctor during the shipping season, they are inspected and stored until called for placement at the Duluth docks. A Proctor Roadswitch or Hill ore assignment takes the trains down the hill to the ore dock for dumping. The trains are left on the ore dock approach and the ore dock switch crew handles the movements for car dumping, either for ground storage or into the pockets for direct loading into a boat.

When a specific cargo of pellets is called for a particular ship, the pellets are returned to the top of the ore dock by a conveyor system. They are then dumped on the special movable conveyor system on the track to the right.

The movable on-track conveyor can handle the pellets from the overhead belt system in the background, and dump into the various pockets designated for the ship load. The pellets in the pockets in the foreground were dumped from ore cars that were spotted, emptied, and removed before the photography session. ALL, DAN MACKEY

The No. 2 ore dock at Two Harbors has been modified with a conveyor belt feeder system as well as the innovative conveyor system loaders.

This view shows all three Two Harbors ore docks, Nos. 1, 2, and 6 (r-to-l). No. 6 is completely disconnected and out of service. Note how No. 2 dock's conveyor chutes extend over the 1000-foot lake boat. The right side still employs gravity chutes for boat loading. The dumping station for pellets is located to the upper right of the storage area (to the left in the photo above the No. 6 dock). The DM&IR is the only railroad that can use both methods of unloading ore cars as well as load vessels with either gravity chutes or the conveyor systems. BOTH, BASGEN PHOTOGRAPHY, DAN MACKEY COLLECTION

On a beautiful fall day in September 1995, three units are handling an empty ore train up the hill toward Proctor, moving slowly in the eighth notch. DAVID C. SCHAUER

When the Proctor Hill ore arrives at the ore dock and cuts off from the train, the crew moves onto the ore dock to pick up a train of empties for movement back to Proctor Yard.

A rear-end device is needed for the Proctor Hill jobs because the air brake systems and the dynamic brakes on the motive power are in heavy use for movement of the 10,000-ton-plus loaded trains down the hill.

The Proctor Hill is a double-track main line and it needs to be for both safety and train traffic density. Proctor Hill crews are assigned on all three shifts, with each crew making from two to three round trips per shift depending on traffic levels.

With four older SD units, a limestone train departs Burlington Northern's yard on Rices Point. Limestone that is not delivered to the DM&IR's dock system or bulk handling facility is delivered to a coal dock adjacent to the DM&IR's ore docks. In this case, the BN (now BNSF) handles the switching at the dock and interchanges with the DM&IR at the Rices Point Yard. Thus one can see BNSF switch engines handling DM&IR ore cars. DAVID C. SCHAUER

This train is in far West Duluth on what is called the Interstate Branch between Adolph and South Itasca. The assignments work out of Proctor and provide interchange service with the BNSF, the Wisconsin Central (CN), and the Soo Line (Canadian Pacific). DAVID C. SCHAUER

An empty ore train departing the Two Harbors yard crosses over the line along the North Shore to Duluth. PATRICK C. DORIN

For just a bit of history back to 1975, the classic DM&IR SD9s and 18s did the switching and placement of the loaded ore cars on the docks. The 180 is about to begin a shove at the Two Harbors yard and docks.

Still another "shove" arrives on dock No. 1.

The tug *Edna G* served the DM&IR's Two Harbors docks for decades. All steamed up, the *Edna G* is about to depart its dock facility to assist the *Presque Isle* to its Dock No. 2 designation. ALL, PATRICK C. DORIN

Proctor yard switch crews make up empty trains for the Range, prepare trains for the trip to the docks, handle yard switching for the local freight trains and transfers to Duluth and the Interstate Branch through Gary-New Duluth, Pokegama and Itasca.

The Duluth facility has had a new job to do since the summer of 1995. Limestone is delivered directly to the storage area to the east of the No. 6 ore dock. It is unloaded from the boats by self-unloading equipment and placed into a receiving bin on the west side of the No. 6 ore dock. It is then moved by a conveyor system for storage until called for movement to a pelletizing plant.

All of the above ores also travel all-rail to steel producing areas.

With the different types of ore, the storage areas are set up to stockpile the pellets separately. Therefore, the products do not get mixed up when the bucket wheel reclaimers begin the process of placing the pellets on the belt system for movement to the ore docks at either Duluth or Two Harbors. This is quite a contrast compared to three decades and nearly a century ago when the railroads had the incredible and complex work of switching and classifying ore shipments according to grade, chemical content, size of the ore (fines, lump, etc.), and boat load specifications.

TYPES OF ORE

The DM&IR once handled nearly two hundred different types of iron ore. Now the company handles but four types of ores, as follows:

Company	Ore Type	Ore Dock Destination
EVTAC	Dry	Duluth
Minorca	Fluxed	Duluth and Two Harbors (Escanaba during winter)
Minntac	Fluxed	Duluth and Two Harbors
Auburn	Natural Ores	Two Harbors

ALL-RAIL ORE MOVEMENTS

The trend on the DM&IR since the 1950s has been a gradual increase in all-rail movements. The term "all-rail" means that the ore is transported by rail exclusively from the mine to the steel plant. During the 1950s, this usually meant a wintertime operation when the Great Lakes were frozen. Since the early 1980s, all-rail traffic has expanded with the movement of iron ores and pellets to far-distant steel producing centers such as Birmingham, Ala., and Geneva, Utah, as well as steel mills in Illinois, Indiana, Ohio, and Pennsylvania. What does this mean in terms of train operations on the DM&IR?

There has been an incredible variety of motive power and types of trains operated for all-rail ore service on the DM&IR. In November 1991, two C&NW units power an all-rail shipment through Iron Junction.
ROBERT C. ANDERSON

C&NW diesel power was common on the DM&IR throughout most of the 1990s including into the Union Pacific era. The ore trains bound for Utah consisted of 100-ton coal hoppers from the UP, C&NW, MP and even later cars from the Rio Grande Railroad. This photo was taken during the summer of 1992.

Jumping forward to January 2001, the Utah-bound trains were led by Union Pacific super power. This three-unit combination has just been delivered to Steelton in far western Duluth. A DM&IR crew will handle the train northward to Adolph and the main line in about an hour. Since it is a late winter day, the sun will be down and the train will depart in North Country darkness.

Yes, Burlington Northern and BNSF ore cars! One hundred twenty cars were in this northbound train. The BNSF delivered the empties to the Steelton Yard just a few hours before photographed en route to Minntac in the late afternoon of August 8, 1998. ALL, PATRICK C. DORIN

The modern all-rail movements have created panorama of train operations. Motive power from the connecting lines for the all-rail run-thrus have included CSX, Wisconsin Central, Union Pacific (including Chicago & North Western, Southern Pacific, and the Rio Grande), and Norfolk Southern. Most of the ore is handled in 100-ton, open-top hopper cars from all of the railroads listed. But this is not all—Burlington Northern (and, later, BNSF) motive power with BN 100-ton ore cars or 100-ton cars from the Bessemer & Lake Erie Railroad are running over the DM&IR for all-rail movements.

Still another variety in the operations are the Minorca trains to Escanaba during the winter season, which operate over the Wisconsin Central from Superior to the Lake Michigan port. These trains consist of the former C&NW ore cars plus repaints and rebuilds for the Wisconsin Central's subsidiary Sault Ste. Marie Bridge Company with SSAM reporting marks. At no other time in the DM&IR's history has there been such a variety in train operations.

MOTIVE POWER

The DM&IR has employed a fleet of Electro-Motive SD types of motive power almost exclusively throughout its diesel-era history. The purpose of this short section is to illustrate and list the various types of motive power, including the various Alcos and power from the B&LE and EJ&E that provided some additional variety throughout the diesel years.

This all-rail empty train was waiting for an Escanaba-bound ore train to be interchanged with the Wisconsin Central at Steelton in January 1998. MICHAEL BURLAGA

No. 321 is a rebuilt SD9, designated SD9M and photographed at Proctor in July 1999. PATRICK C. DORIN

EMD SD9s were once the mainstay of DM&IR motive power. Duluth, September 1980. THOMAS DORIN

DM&IR's SD9s with steam generators, Nos. 129 and 130, were leased by Amtrak for service on its Duluth trains, as here on February 5, 1977. PATRICK C. DORIN

The DM&IR also operated a fleet of EMD SD18s. THOMAS DORIN

The DM&IR's ex-Union Pacific Alco C-630s retained their UP paint with black "DMIR" reporting marks. Proctor, July 1974. PATRICK C. DORIN

A rebuilt SD9 with a new low nose, No. 163, is shoving a group of rebuilt ore cars for pellet traffic on the Duluth docks. "Slug" No. 500 ahead is a power unit with traction motors on the trucks but without a diesel engine. The 500 drew its power from the 163. TIM SCHANDEL

The SD38s, with 2000 horsepower, were part of the next step in DM&IR motive power history. SD38DC No. 233 is shown here between assignments at the Proctor roundhouse in July 1999. PATRICK C. DORIN

This rear view of SD38DC No. 221 at Proctor in July 1999 shows the placement of the bell and the paint scheme arrangement around the rear of the hood. PATRICK C. DORIN

One of the SD38s was repainted with the ISO 9002 symbol and renumbered 9002. Also, the "M" in Missabe is styled like the University of Minnesota's "M". The 9002 was the lead unit for an all-rail empty ore train for the Mesabi Range ready to depart Steelton on a beautiful winter day in early 1998. MICHAEL BURLAGA

The DM&IR leased power from its sister railroads from time to time, such as this Bessemer & Lake Erie SD38, No. 892, handling the DM&IR's Miscellaneous Road Freight. PATRICK C. DORIN

SD38 No. 207, handling a transfer, is shown here just west of the Duluth ore docks. St. Louis Bay is in the background as well as the coal terminal on the Superior side of the bay. DAVID C. SCHAUER

A group of 400-series units on the DM&IR are classified as SD40-3s. A new step forward for the SD40 group, these units are rebuilt "tunnel motors" from the Southern Pacific. The 404 is leading a train at Waldo in July 1998. David C. Schauer

DM&IR DIESEL MOTIVE POWER ROSTER

Type	Builder	Series	H.P.	Remarks
SW9	EMD	11 to 25	1200	Built in 1953, all switch engines were sold by 1963
NW2	EMD	11 (2nd)	1200	Ex-EJ&E 455, purchased in 1998. Built in 1949
RSD-15	Alco	50 to 55	2400	Built in 1959, sold to B&LE in 1964.
SD9	EMD	100 to 174	1750	Built 1956-1959. All sold or converted to SD-Ms
SD18	EMD	175 to 193	1800	All sold or converted to SD-Ms
SD38AC	EMD	200 to 208	2000	Built in 1971
SD38-2	EMD	209 -213, 215 9002	2000	Built in 1975 Ex-211, renumbered 9002 in 1998.
SD38DC	EMD	214, 216 217 221-223, 225	2000	Built 1967 and 1970
SD-M		301 to 322		Rebult SD9s and SD18s
SD40-3		400 to 419	3000	Rebuilt SD45T-2s, except former SD45-2s. 416 and 418
C-630	Alco	900 to 909	3000	Ex Union Pacific 2900-2909, built in 1966. Purchased by DM&IR in 1973 and all sold by 1976.
Slug		500		Operated as slug with SD9 163 in 1988.

Notes: SD9s 129 and 130 equipped with steam generator for passenger service.
SD18 No. 193 was converted to a low nose in 1992 and donated to the Lake Superior Railroad Museum in 1998.
Roster in 2001 included the SD38s in the 200 and 300 series, and the SD40-3s in the 400 series, plus NW2 No. 11.

DM&IR 29165 is the basic type of ore car operated by the company, as well as the other Minnesota ore lines. Designated the "Minnesota Ore Car," they have different dimensions than the Michigan cars with the same 70-75 ton capacities. As of 2001, the DM&IR still operated over 1500 such cars without extensions. Although barely visible, the capacity tonnage is located at the upper left-hand corner of the car. PATRICK C. DORIN

This photo shows three of the crude ore cars—45015, 40729, and 40738—mixed in with a group of ballast cars rebuilt from various ore car groups. The cars were in service when photographed at Keenan in August 1999. PATRICK C. DORIN

THE DM&IR ORE, FREIGHT, AND PASSENGER CAR FLEETS

The DM&IR maintains a substantial fleet of 24-foot ore cars. Through the rebuilding process, the company has an interesting variety of ore cars in operation. New ore car designs were under consideration in 2001 for operation on the ore docks in Duluth and Two Harbors.

The commercial freight car fleet reflects the mining company and wood products needs of the North Country. For the past few years, the DM&IR owned three passenger cars for use as a business train. The complete roster included a combination car, a former Northern Pacific *North Coast Limited* coach and the DM&IR's business car *Northland*.

The ex-NP coach was donated to the Lake Superior Railroad Museum in 2000. The company also borrows other equipment, such as DM&IR coach No. 33 and others, from the Museum when additional capacity is needed for particular special train. The DM&IR train belong to the "classic trains" category in ever sense of the term.

TACONITE: TONNAGE AND TRENDS

The DM&IR serves three taconite plants wit the following potential annual production capac ities:

EVTAC	5.6 million tons
MINNTAC	15.8 million tons
MINORCA	2.7 million tons

Not including any natural ores, the railroa has the potential traffic level of 24.1 million tor of pellets if the companies are operating at capac ity. This is approximately 50% of the record tor nages during the early 1950s of over 50 millio tons for all types of ores.

Over the same approximate period DM&IR route mileage dropped from 560 mile in 1960 to 192 miles as of January 2001.

It goes without saying that the Duluth Missabe & Iron Range Railway is a remarkabl railroad. It is a small company, which in tur provides a sense of community, but at the sam time plays a crucial role in the economy of Nort America—the movement of iron ore fror Northern Minnesota for the production of ste products for consumers throughout the conti nent, and around the world. Hats off to a super railroad company!

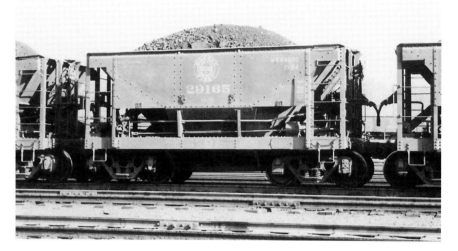

Car 32405 illustrates the high-level air brake hoses applied by the DM&IR so crews could couple hoses without bending down between the wheels of the close-coupled cars.

Car 60943 is part of the largest number series (60000-61140) without extensions—970 cars were on the roster as of May 2001.

Car 60285 shows its B-end at Proctor Yard in 1997.

Car 52614, at Proctor in 1979, is one of the fleet rebuilt with the 9-3/4-inch extensions.

Crude ore cars like 40428 transport raw taconite ore to the pelletizing plants. Extensions are 19-1/2 inches, with slots for the car shakers.
ALL, PATRICK C. DORIN

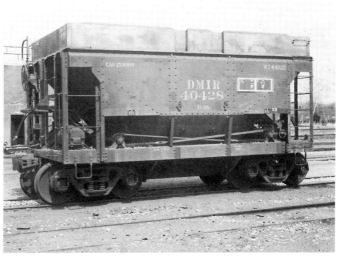

These rebuilt cars are known as mini-quads: the extension is much smaller than the former 16- or 18-inch extensions, and the cars are semi-permanently coupled in four-car sets. Orange stripes on the corners designate the coupler ends. Proctor, 1979.

These two cars were among those modified for ballast service.

The DM&IR rebuilt a total of 102 ore cars for ballast service, with 14-inch extensions and four ballast hopper doors. They are painted yellow with maroon lettering.

At least two DM&IR ore cars were rebuilt for locomotive sand service, such as No. W24456 in maroon paint at Keenan in August 1998. ALL, PATRICK C. DORIN

The DM&IR has remodeled three ore cars for a variety of tests including the hopper doors, brake systems, and a variety of other functions. The cars were painted white, maroon, and blue. The trio was photographed in operation on the rear of a loaded train near Spirit Mountain headed for the ore docks. DAVID C. SCHAUER

Covered hopper car 4987 (4981-4987) was operated "For Dried Sand Only." The car was painted maroon with gold lettering. PATRICK C. DORIN

Gondola 87663 was part of a group of 15 cars leased from the Elgin, Joliet & Eastern Railway for general freight service on the DM&IR. The cars were painted black with white lettering. PATRICK C. DORIN

Gondola 3655 has been rebuilt with bulkheads at each end for pulpwood traffic. The car was painted maroon with gold lettering. PATRICK C. DORIN

Gondola 4237 has a different type of rib arrangement, not extending to the bottom of the car, but rather to the floor line. The car was loaded with wheels and freight car trucks when photographed with a group of ore cars. PATRICK C. DORIN

33

The DM&IR's business car is appropriately named *Northland*.

The W-24 is a combination car operated as part of the DM&IR's classic business car group. It is not only operated in DM&IR trains, but also in Lake Superior Railroad Museum specials, such as the D&NE train in 1973. The car has run on the BN and the DW&P in a variety of specials operated for mining engineers, railfans, and company trips for shippers and inspection runs.

The DM&IR purchased a streamlined coach from the Northern Pacific for part of their special passenger car fleet, naming it *Minnesota II*.

What better way to end this chapter on the DM&IR than with a photo of the end of a taconite ore train from Minntac at the inbound yard at Two Harbors? Modern extended-vision cabooses such as the C-237 were still part of the operation when this scene was recorded in 1975.
ALL, PATRICK C. DORIN

DULUTH, MISSABE & IRON RANGE RAILWAY
REPRESENTATIVE ORE CAR ROSTERS

1970s—

The dimensions for the following groups of ore cars are as follows:

24 feet coupled length

10 feet, 8 7/8 inches extreme width

10 feet, 2 inches extreme height

Class	Number Series	Cars on Roster 1973	Built
U17	23975 to 24999	572	1937-38
U18	25000 to 25499	243	1942
U19	25500 to 25999	483	1942
U20	26000 to 26499	469	1942
U22	27000 to 27499	359	1943
U23	27500 to 27999	482	1948
U24	28000 to 28499	484	1948
U25	28500 to 28999	490	1948
U26	29000 to 29499	479	1948
U27	29500 to 30499	958	1949
U28	30500 to 30999	480	1949
U29	31000 to 32499	1446	1952
U30	32500 to 32999	299	1953
U27-U31	50031 to 59991	94	Converted with high sides (19-1/2" extensions) during the period 1964 to 1969. The side extensions were equipped with shaker pockets
U30-U31	52500 to 53498	652	Converted to mini-quads 1971-1973 with 9-1/2 inch side extensions.

The year 2000 DM&IR roster included the following ore cars—

Class	Number Series	No. of Cars	Remarks
U23	27504 to 27997	96	
U24	28010 to 28486	60	
U25	28505 to 28996	58	
U26	29000 to 29495	107	
U27	29504 to 30499	183	
U28	30501 to 30999	136	
U29	31036 to 32475	41	
254	60000 to 61140	970	Numbers vary within this group.
U29 U30 U31	51000 to 53498	1640	Mini-quads
	40316-40797	264	Crude ore cars
	49001-49008		Numbers vary within this group.

2 FROM GN AND NP T

ABOVE: The BNSF rebuilt over 200 cars in 1998 with covers for a special iron ore traffic in the south that never materialized. The cars returned to Superior, Wisconsin for regular ore service without the covers, in the series 600000 to 600374. Note the end extension at both ends of the car, added to eliminate spillage. ROBERT BLOMQUIST

FACING PAGE: This Great Northern publicity photo tells it all about the ore trains during the 1950s and 1960s on the "Big G." Three F-units in perfect harmony powered trains ranging in length from 180 to 220 cars. This loaded train's portrait was taken from the U.S. 2 overpass near Brookston, Minnesota. The train is eastbound on the Mesabi Division's Third Subdivision. GREAT NORTHERN, PATRICK C. DORIN COLLECTION

Many changes took place in Minnesota's ore country between 1966 and 1996. Two very famous and customer-oriented railroads, the Great Northern and the Northern Pacific, merged with the Chicago Burlington & Quincy and the Spokane Portland & Seattle to form Burlington Northern. Major planning for this merger took place during the 1960s with the actual merger taking place in March 1970. Twenty-six years later, the BN and the Santa Fe joined forces as Burlington Northern Santa Fe, with the new reporting marks BNSF.

Most of the historical coverage in this chapter covers the Burlington Northern since its formation through 1995. The BNSF took up the task in 1996 with the beginning of a new era in ore hauling.

The BN handled iron ore not only in

BNSF

Moving forward to the Burlington Northern era, F-units continued to work the ore trains. This photo could be a composite history with F9 No. 9800 leading two B-units in the Big Sky Blue and the Pullman Green and Omaha Orange with a Blue GN F7. The train itself is made up of repainted BN ore cars mixed with former GN cars, and is departing the former Butler Taconite Plant at Nashwauk. Both the GN and BN operated quartets of F-units on the "tac" trains during the late 1960s and into the early 1970s.
PATRICK C. DORIN

the Lake Superior region but over a wide geographic area. Most of the traffic was hauled relatively short distances, i.e., from the Mesabi Range to the Allouez ore dock facilities over the Great Northern's Mesabi Division. There was, however, some interesting all-rail traffic to Gary, Indiana; Birmingham, Alabama; Granite City, Illinois; and several Ohio and Pennsylvania steel mill destinations.

THE WORLD-FAMOUS MESABI RANGE

There were several natural iron ore mines operating on the Mesabi, which required extensive switching and other services at the time of the Burlington Northern merger. At the same time, there were only two taconite pelletizing plants a Nashwauk and Keewatin.

These two plants were served by unit train made up of ex-Great Northern and Northern Pacific 75-ton capacity ore cars with 20-inch side extensions. For the most part, each plant wa served by one train on an every-other-day basis The single daily train of 200 cars would run from the pellet storage yard at Allouez to one o the plants, load, and return to home base. The train would run through the dumper upon arrival, be inspected and prepared for the next day's run. The pellets would be stockpiled on the ground to await the arrival of a boat.

The natural ore picture was different. The entire period of time for the natural ore operations was one of decline for the BN. This continued until 1987 when it was completely eliminated from the picture.

Switching back to the 1960s and 1970s, the mining companies would indicate the number o loads for a particular boat each 24-hour period The GN, and later the BN, would assemble enough empty ore cars in anticipation of these requirements, and route them to the "Range" in ore extras. These trains would deliver the empties to various yards including Kelly Lake, Calumet and Canisteo. From these points, the road crews would continue on and pick up loaded ore cars from one or more of the various small yards of sidings between Kelly Lake and Gunn. The trains would then return to Allouez as had been the operation since the 1890s on the Great Northern.

The shaded area on this Burlington Northern map illustrates most of the Mesabi Range, measuring approximately 100 miles long and between 1-1/2 and 3 miles wide. Also shown is former Great Northern trackage and the location of the three taconite plants and mines served by the Burlington Northern.
BN, PATRICK C. DORIN COLLECTION

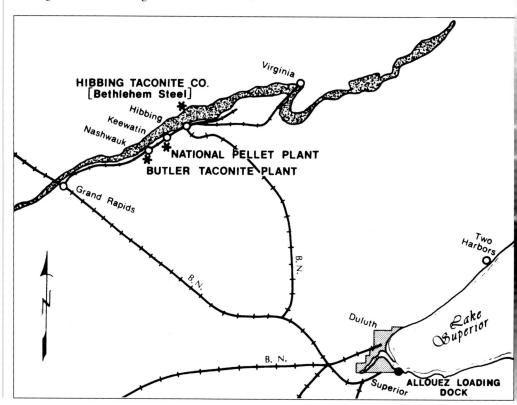

Upon arrival in Allouez, the train would be inspected for any problems. A yard assignment would then push the train over the Allouez dump while weighing the individual loads at the same time. The loads were classified as to the type of ore as well as for particular boat loads according to the specifications of the steel company purchasing the ore.

The loaded cars were then stored in the yard until called for by the dock agent. Ore yard crews worked with two SD7s or SD9s. The cars would be assembled for movement onto a specific ore dock and placement for unloading. When assembled, the crew would pull—yes, pull—the loads out of the yard and run up the approach to the three ore docks. Upon arrival at the dock area,

This train at the National plant at Keewatin, Minn., was typical of those operated prior to the purchase of 100-ton capacity cars, and displayed a bit of diversity with the mixture of GN and BN ore cars.
BURLINGTON NORTHERN,
PATRICK C. DORIN COLLECTION

As history moved on through the 1970s, the F-units were replaced with GP38s and GP38-2s on the ore trains. In this case, a Butler tac train is rolling by the DM&IR's Marble/Calumet, Minnesota, station on joint DM&IR/BN trackage. Four GP38s are powering the 200 loads on March 19, 1978, as the train heads for Gunn, where it will turn eastward to Superior. The Butler plant is no longer in operation, but consideration has been given to converting the former mine area into a modern steel plant.
ROBERT C. ANDERSON

Into the 1980s, the GP38 groups were replaced by SD40s and SD40-2s like No. 6022 West passing the old Saunders Tower south of Superior. This particular train was an example of the transition era in the 1980s. The front section of the train consisted of the new 100-ton capacity ore cars. The second segment included the rebuilt 75-ton cars with the extensions on both BN and GN cars. The final segment was a mixture of 13 former NP and GN cars without extensions.
PATRICK C. DORIN

the engines would cut off, run through a crossover to the adjacent approach track, and back down toward the ore yard until reaching another crossover on the lower end of the approach. Changing tracks again, the crew would return to the train, couple up and complete the "shove" on the designated dock, One, Two or Four. Once the train was spotted over the assigned pockets, the crew would pick up empties and return to the ore yard. The bad-order cars would then be switched out, with the remaining cars brought to the outbound yard for assembly into a train for the Range.

The BN method of moving ore to the ore docks was completely different from the Great Northern operation. The GN shoved the loaded cars to the docks with one SD unit.

The number of ore extras for natural ore declined from about three or four per day to one per day by the end of the 1970s, and finally less than daily. From 1979 on, all natural ore traffic was interchanged with the DM&IR at Wilpen, Minnesota. This eliminated the need for extensive dock operations for the small amount of iron ore, and also provided the mining companies with more frequent service from the DM&IR. Such ore was dumped on the DM&IR docks in Duluth.

The Burlington Northern's operations on the range also dwindled. In the early 1970s, there

With two SD40-2s and one SD9 for power, a tac train departs Allouez for Hibbing Taconite in mid-1989. One-hundred-ton capacity cars now make up the complete consist of the tac trains for the Mesabi Range.

The SD9 was set out at Kelly Lake and the tac train continued on its journey to the Hib Tac plant.

Cabooses were still part of the consist for this 140 car train.

The train is now in the loading process which will take about two hours. ALL, PATRICK C. DORIN

were mine-run crews operating around the clock on a daily basis. By the end of the decade, the operations were no longer around the clock; and in some cases not even on a daily basis. The business of distributing empty ore cars to the various mines and picking up loads from the mines and ore washing plants was rapidly becoming an operation of the past. The new and larger taconite plants, with their uniform pellet product, did not require switching or classification and the unit trains simply load, run and dump.

Originally, the BN operated one taconite train (known as "tac trains") per day to the range. This number doubled when the taconite plant at Hibbing was placed in operation in 1976. For a nine-year period, the BN served the three plants at Nashwauk, Keewatin and Hibbing. The Butler Plant at Nashwauk shut down in 1985, leaving only two plants shipping on the BN through 2001. (There has been talk about plans to reopen the mine at Nashwauk and build a steel plant at the site. This will add a new component for the BNSF operations.)

The number of road trains to the Range can vary from one to three per day depending upon all-rail movements. The all-rail trains' empties either originate at Allouez or run directly from their all-rail operation from the Twin Cities line depending upon the type of train, such as an interchange movement to the DM&IR at Steelton. Returning loaded all-rail trains turn south at Boylston, the junction with the line to the Twin Cities.

Three GP38s, led by the 2100, roll around the curve after leaving the main line at Saunders. Just a few more miles to go and the train will arrive at Allouez. The bay window caboose was the only type of caboose that would clear the loading facilities after the last car of the train was loaded (on the move) at the two plants at Nashwauk and Keewatin. BOTH, ROBERT BLOMQUIST

Three SD40-2s were common for many of the tac trains during the 1980s and 1990s. Burlington Northern No. 7291 is leading a trio powering an empty train bound for the Hib Tac plant during a summer evening in 1985. PATRICK C. DORIN

Caboose 10506 brings up the rear of 7291 West, as it is identified by the dispatcher. PATRICK C. DORIN

It is June 17, 2000, and the BNSF is operating SD60M's on the ore trains. This empty Hib Tac has reached the end of the double track at milepost 15.9, which is west of the junction (Boylston) of the Twin Cities and the line west to the Mesabi Range and North Dakota. ROBERT BLOMQUIST

THE ALLOUEZ TACONITE FACILITY

The Allouez ore dock and pellet storage facility is a major component of the logistics from the mines/pellet plants to the steel producers. The facility dumps the ore cars, stores the pellets, and provides the ore dock with the appropriate tonnages for the Great Lakes ships.

Before getting into the Allouez operations, there is an interesting story about a foreign exchange student in the Twin Ports. She was nearing the end of her stay, which she had enjoyed a great deal. She also enjoyed tacos.

For many years there had been a sign at the entrance to Allouez, bearing the word "Taconite." This piece of English was interpreted as a taco restaurant with a name meaning "Taco Night Restaurant." The student told her host family that she wanted to eat at the "TacoNite Resturant." They were quite puzzled because

The Allouez taconite storage area and yard is located on the far east side of Superior, Wisconsin. The pellets are transported from ore cars to the designated storage area by conveyor belts, and then piled high with the stacker to await loading into lake boats.
BURLINGTON NORTHERN,
PATRICK C. DORIN COLLECTION

Although ore dock "shoves" and switching are now a chapter of the past at Allouez, the BN (BNSF) still operates yard assignments there for train assembly, switching out bad-order equipment, and for the movement of cars between Allouez and the main freight yard at 28th Street. These two SD9s (ex-Great Northern) are resting between assignments by the yard tower in Allouez. PATRICK C. DORIN

Allouez Yard is the receiving point for inbound BNSF dock trains, which use these two dumping facilities. BOTH, PATRICK C. DORIN

As the ore cars are emptied, the pellets are transferred by conveyor belt to the appropriate storage areas to await movement to the ore dock for boat loading. Note the various stockpiles in the background. BURLINGTON NORTHERN, PATRICK C. DORIN COLLECTION

they had never heard of such a name in Duluth-Superior. They went for a drive so that the student could show them where it was located, and had quite a laugh when they discovered it was how she interpreted the sign for the BN taconite facility. Needless to say, they returned to Duluth and went to Taco Johns for a special treat and "Mexican" delight.

The Allouez facility had its beginning under the direction of the Great Northern Railway. The operation of the then new storage facility and conveyor belt system began in 1967. The storage area was as large as 32 football fields and could store 2.2 million tons of pellets. Ore dock No. 1 was modified so that all of the 374 pockets could be fed by the conveyor system for boat loading. This operation was originally designed for the Nashwauk and Keewatin plants and continued through to the 1990s. However, dock No. 1 has been out of service for over ten years as of this writing in 2002.

The Burlington Northern expanded the Allouez facility in 1977, just ten years after the original system was placed in operation by the

For many years, the old Great Northern No. 1 ore dock was also fed by a conveyor system for transloading to ore boats, as in this August 1974 view. JEFFREY LEMKE

reat Northern. The No. 5 ore dock was built ith a conveyor feeder system, 36 storage silos, 30 feet high and 900 feet long—bin-to-bin (silo silo) length; and it can handle 1000-foot-long ke carriers. The ore boats are loaded from a ries of 18 rectractable conveyors, one for each ir of bins. They are mounted 45 feet above the ater line and can be extended 65 feet out over e boat to load the pellets. A 1000-foot super rrier can be loaded with as much as 58,000 ns in a four- to five-hour period.

The first boat to load at the new ore dock as the *Harry Allen*, owned by the S&E Ship- ng Corporation of Cleveland, Ohio. It took on 1,565 tons on June 8, 1977. On June 21 of the me year, a record boat load for the Head of the akes was taken on by the *Mesabi Miner*, one of e then new 1000-foot ore carriers owned by terlake Steamship Company. The total tonnage this new record set in 1977 was 56,200 tons.

The ore dock is a major landmark in the Superior area. It was the first new ore dock built on Lake Superior since the Erie and Reserve Mining Companies completed their docks in the 1950s at Taconite Harbor and Silver Bay. With the outside storage areas, the BN (now BNSF) has a highly efficient bulk handling system with a high ore car utilization factor as well as providing an ore storage service for the steel companies.

In addition to the car dumpers, stackers, and bucket wheel reclaimers, the BNSF also maintains a minor repair facility for ore cars, dock and yard offices, weighing facilities (both rail and conveyor belt systems) and an ore testing office. The latter samples pellets to determine quality, chemical content, etc. Yard trackage includes two loop tracks for the car dumping, and tracks for both inbound and outbound ore trains, storage of yard motive power, ore cars, and work equipment.

The conveyor system handled the pellets to the top of the dock. The top dock machinery or dumper was flexible and distributed pellets in the pockets on both sides of the ore dock. Note the pellets on the conveyor belt as well as in the pockets on the right side of the dock. PATRICK C. DORIN

The old Great Northern No. 2 ore dock. The remaining GN docks, Nos. 2 and 4, were never modified with conveyor belts for the taconite facilities. Widening of U.S. 2 through Superior required the dismantling of the railroad approach to the docks 1, 2 and 4; and subsequently Nos. 2 and 4 can no longer handle iron ore shipments. PATRICK C. DORIN

This photo of a tac train ready to depart from Allouez is another example of the transition era. The tac trains have a relatively simple and effective operation. Departing Allouez, they run to the designated mine and plant, load, and return to Allouez, usually within 12 hours. The trains can literally make a round trip each day. Patrick C. Dorin

The No. 5 ore dock is fed by conveyor belts. Conveyor belt loading chutes can move out over the bigger and wider 1000-foot ore carriers for a very effective loading procedure. Although hidden in the shadows, one chute has moved out over the boat just ahead of the boat's self-unloading mechanism. Basgen Photography, Patrick C. Dorin Collection

By 2001, the three remaining pocket ore docks were inactive. No. 1 is still connected with a conveyor system and could be reactivated should traffic levels dictate. Ore docks 2 and 4 are disconnected from the railroad approach. When the State of Wisconsin widened U.S. Route 2 through Allouez, the dock approach bridge over the highway was removed. It cut off the possibility of using Nos. 2 and 4 for rail dumping of iron ore, pellets, or the shipment of potash or even coal. With the dismantling of this short section of the rail approach to the ore docks, a great deal of flexibility was lost.

ALL-RAIL AND OTHER ORE BUSINESS

During the time period from 1970 through the 2002, the all-rail ore train services have increased in importance. The process once was only a "winter" operation when the lakes were frozen and ore was needed at the steel mills. Now, it is a year-round operation, and some of the destinations include St. Louis, the Chicago area, Birmingham, Alabama (known as Fairfield trains), and Pennsylvania.

There have been some interesting developments in the all-rail business. Since some of the all-rail traffic is loaded at Minntac on the DM&IR, the BNSF now interchanges the trains at Steelton (far western Duluth). BNSF motive power and the equipment is then handled by DM&IR crews to Minntac and return (see Chapter 1).

The consists of the all-rail ore trains include the BN/BNSF ore cars, but in many cases, there are cars lettered for Bessemer & Lake Erie, CSX, Rio Grande (UP) and other carriers depending upon the destination of the ore train. Ex-Frisco ore cars have also been part of the consist of many all-rail ore trains. Train lengths can range from as few as 50 cars to over 100 depending upon the destination, the need, and other circumstances surrounding a particular shipment or train. The frequency of all-rail trains can vary

A classic A-B-A F-unit set leads an empty all-rail movement into the siding at Cambridge, Minnesota, in July 1976 to meet the southbound Amtrak passenger train from Duluth to the Twin Cities. PATRICK C. DORIN

General Electric U-Boats not only handled the Mesabi Range dock trains, but also the all-rails. BN U25C 5606 leads another U-Boat still in the Burlington Route scheme on an empty train of mostly GN ore cars through Minneapolis and headed for the "North Country" on July 1, 1973. EDWARD L. KANAK

There is not much snow on the ground even though it is February 24, 1974. Three U-Boats led by the 5603 are handling over 100 DM&IR loaded ore cars for Gary, Indiana. The train was eastbound through Minneapolis. EDWARD L. KANAK

Motive power mixes knew no limits on the BN all-rail ore trains. An ex-Great Northern F45 leads two SD45s through Dayton's Bluff, southeast of downtown St. Paul on August 24, 1974. This westbound freight from Chicago is handling empty ore cars for the Mesabi Range as well as piggyback and regular freight. Sometimes as the empty ore cars were delivered back to the BN, they would be forwarded back to Northern Minnesota in the regular freight trains like this one. WILLIAM S. KUBA

SD40-2s were also part of the motive power assignments for all-rail ore trains during the 1970s. An empty ore train with a mixture of 100 former GN and NP ore cars moves northward through Cambridge, Minnesota. PATRICK C. DORIN

It is February 1978, with plenty of snow on the ground on the western end of the Mesabi Range. A loaded all-rail ore from the Butler plant rolls along near Nashwauk, Minnesota. Again the consist is a mixture of GN and NP ore cars without extensions. ROBERT C. ANDERSON

It is foggy and humid for a September 1980 day in the Northland as three SD40-2s lead an all-rail ore around the curve at Boylston from the line to Grand Forks to the Twin Cities line. Again the consist of the train includes a mixture of GN and NP 24-foot ore cars. PATRICK C. DORIN

As the train rolled around the curve, its identification changed from Extra 8124 East to Extra 8124 West as it moved toward Minneapolis and St. Paul. Upon reaching the Twin Cities, it would again become Extra 8124 East for its run down the main line next to the Mississippi River. A BN wide-vision cupola caboose brought up the rear of this tac train. PATRICK C. DORIN

All-rail Extra 6927 East is running north over the former Northern Pacific tracks between St. Paul and Hinckley, Minnesota, in June 1978. The motive power consist includes BN 6927 plus a Southern Pacific "Tunnel Motor" and a DM&IR SD9. The train was rolling over the main line at North Branch, Minnesota, with 180 empties. PATRICK C. DORIN

This train is an all-rail empty ore train consisting entirely of the 100-ton capacity ore cars. The train was en route from Granite City, Illinois, back to the Mesabi Range and passing through LaCrosse, Wisconsin, on the former CB&Q main line on May 21, 1988. WILLIAM S. KUBA

Moving into the BNSF era, the all-rail ore trains were again powered by green and orange motive power. An empty Fairfield all-rail arrives at Saunders in May 2001 and will soon be turning on the Milwaukee Connection and heading for the DM&IR's Steelton Yard in Gary-New Duluth. The train will travel to Minntac over the DM&IR with the BNSF power. Although the loaded train will not travel over the Bessemer & Lake Erie Railroad to its Birmingham, Alabama, destination, the train consists of many B&LE 100-ton capacity hopper cars. PATRICK C. DORIN

This BNSF all-rail loaded train is approaching Boylston on June 17, 2000, and will soon be making the swing to the south for movement toward the Twin Cities.
ROBERT BLOMQUIST

Who would have thought that Santa Fe motive power would someday power all-rail ore trains over the former Great Northern trackage? This all-rail empty train is heading for the Mesabi Range to be loaded with taconite pellets for shipment to Birmingham, Alabama. The train is about to depart the 28th Street Yard in Superior. It will travel south to Saunders, then switch over to the DM&IR's Interstate Branch. The train will operate over the DM&IR to the Minntac Plant at Mountain Iron for its load of U.S. Steel pellets. This adds even more diversity to the DM&IR consists. ROBERT BLOMQUIST

The Northern Pacific operated a fleet of GP7s, GP9s, and Alco RS-11s in its ore train operations and pool service with the Soo Line. Note the mixture of the EMD and Alco power and the Soo Line ore car in this view. PATRICK C. DORIN COLLECTION

The majority of the ore cars on hand at the Burlington Northern merger were from the Great Northern fleet. Note the rivets on the rectangular side of car 91346. PATRICK C. DORIN

from one or two within 24 hours to as few as one per week. Again it depends upon shipper consignee requirements.

THE FORMER NORTHERN PACIFIC ORE LINES

Before closing this chapter on train operations, we need to take a quick look at the former Northern Pacific operations on the Cuyuna Range at Ironton, Minnesota.

This route was a minor contributor to the BN ore traffic levels. In fact, although there had been a number of trains to the BN docks in t[he] early 1970s, both from the former NP and S[oo] Line; by 1980 the ore traffic for the NP lines ha[d] died completely. The Soo Line continued [to] operate solid ore trains to and from the Cuyu[na] Range, which were delivered to the BN's Allou[ez] Yard until 1980. From that time on, the S[oo] Line interchanged their ore trains with t[he] DM&IR for dumping on the Duluth docks.

In terms of ore tonnage, Burlington Nort[h]ern was securing less than 30,000 tons of o[re] annually during the last years. The Cuyu[na] Range once provided the former NP ore do[ck] with a 3-million-ton annual traffic level.

The Northern Pacific dock stands alone [on] the Allouez Bay without its rail approach. It is [a] sad reminder of the once-glorious days of iron o[re] railroading on the Northern Pacific.

On the other hand, BNSF operates hea[vy] coal traffic over the former NP main line throu[gh] the Cuyuna Range. Tonnage over the Tw[in] Ports–Staples line is the highest it has ever been.

ORE HAULING EQUIPMENT

The BN converted the GN and NP ore car flee[t] with 20-inch side extensions for handling pelle[ts.] During the 1980s, the company began investi[ng] in a fleet of 100-ton-capacity, 35-foot ore ca[rs] which completely replaced the 24-foot ore ca[rs.] As of 2002, the 100-ton cars comprised thr[ee]

Great Northern ore car 94112, before it went to scrap. Note the shape of the end sill above the coupler. ROBERT BLOMQUIST

Great Northern 87195 is one of the tapered-side fleet. MICHAEL DORIN

Only four ore cars without extensions got BN lettering. No. 78519 is ex-NP. The others were 78316, 78327, and 78323.

BN 95590 is ex-GN. GN, NP, and Soo once ran over 10,000 ore cars in the Allouez operations. By 1991, less than 150 of the 24-foot cars were left on BN. BN rebuilt much of this fleet with 20-inch extensions.

BN 96004 is a former NP car with 20-inch extensions. No NP cars were rebuilt with extensions prior to the merger. The last group of NP ore cars had smooth sides with squared ends. PATRICK C. DORIN

When the BN merged with the Frisco in 1980, the company acquired a group of ore cars in the 180000-180098 series with 38' 8" coupled length. Originally, the cars were operated for imported Venezuelan ore service via the port of Mobile, Alabama. The ore was handled northward from Mobile to Amory, and then moved eastward to a connection with the Birmingham Southern Railroad for delivery. The cars were operated by BN in all-rail service from the Mesabi Range.

The ex-Frisco fleet was repainted and renumbered as BN series 543000-543098. The paint scheme was box car red with white lettering.

Other all-rail ore equipment included series 551000-551520 (48 feet, 9 inches long and 12 feet, 4 inches high). No. 551398 was at Boylston in 1991.

BN purchased 200, 100-ton capacity ore cars from Bethlehem in 1976. Car 99103 was part of the series 99000-99199.

Car No. 99310 shows the original lettering scheme for this series as well as the final design of cars without the extensions as shown on the 99103. The 99300-99399 group was built by Pacific Car and Foundry. ALL, PATRICK C. DORIN

BN 99464 (99400-99699) was part of the next group of 300 cars built by Bethlehem Johnstown in 1980. Note the yellow striping at the right end. PATRICK C. DORIN

Close-up of 99732, a "B" car. Note the white striping on the corner posts, indicating the couplers. The set was numbered as follows: 99732 B, 99733 C, 99734 C, and 99735 A. ROBERT BLOMQUIST

As the DM&IR converted part of its taconite ore car fleet to "quads," BN purchased a new set of 100-ton cars, also called "quads." Numbered 99700 to 99799, the cars were numbered with letter suffixes: A, C, C, B. The A and B cars are end cars with standard couplers. BN purchased 25 four-car sets. ROBERT BLOMQUIST

BN 99863 was part of series 99800-99949, built in 1988 by Bethlehem Johnstown. PAT DORIN

BN/BNSF AND PREDECESSOR ORE CAR ROSTER SUMMARIES

The following tables list the ore car fleets of the BN/BNSF, and the last listings for the GN and NP.

Table I — 100-Ton Capacity Ore Cars
Burlington Northern
Burlington Northern Santa Fe

Car Numbers	Year Built	Qty	Builder
99000 to 99399	1976	400	Bethlehem Steel Pacific Car and Foundry (200 each)
99400 to 99699	1980	300	Bethlehem Johnstown
99700 to 99799	1981	100	Bethlehem Johnstown In groups of 4 called "Quads" (25 sets)
99800 to 99949	1988	150	Bethlehem Johnstown
98000 to 98099	1992	100	Johnstown America
98100 to 98189	1995	90	Johnstown America

Ordered by BNSF

Car Numbers	Year Built	Qty	Builder
601090 to 601179	1996	90	Johnstown America With TSM Electric Brake System
601180 to 601399	1998	220	Johnstown America With New York Electric brake system
600000 to 600374	1998	230	Cars rebuilt from groups constructed in 1976-1980. Covers were removed in cars placed back in service for the Mesabi Range.

Table II — Burlington Northern "Minnesota" Ore Cars for Taconite Service

Car Numbers	Former Numbers	
95006 to 95037	GN 95006 to 95037	
95500 to 95839	GN 95500 to 95839	
95840 to 96043	NP 77800 to 77999	Last NP cars built - Constructed with square corners
96044 to 96085	GN 93500 to 94199	

Table III — Representative Northern Pacific Railway Roster (70/75-Ton Capacity Cars)

Car Numbers	Year	Qty	Remarks
77800 to 77999	1957	200	Built by NP at Brainerd - See Table II
78000 to 78199	1924	200	Pressed Steel Car Company
78300 to 78499	1950	200	Northern Pacific at Brainerd
78500 to 78699	1952	200	Northern Pacific at Brainerd
78700 to 78899	1954	200	Northern Pacific at Brainerd

Cars 78000 to 78899 are very close to the Walthers HO scale model.

BN/BNSF AND PREDECESSOR ORE CAR ROSTER SUMMARIES (cont'd)

Table IV - Representative Great Northern Ore Car Roster (70/75-Ton Capacity Cars)

Number Series	Built	Qty	Remarks
85500 to 85800	1930	301	Built by Great Northern at Superior
86210 to 86499	1929	290	Built by Standard Steel Car
86500 to 86999	1925	500	Built by Bethlehem Steel Company
89000 to 89749	1923	750	Built by Pressed Steel Car Company
90000 to 93499	1937	3450	Several companies
	1942		
93500 to 94199	1952	700	ACF
95000 to 95039		40	Rebuilt by GN with 18 inch extensions
95500 to 95719		220	Rebuilt by GN with 20 inch extensions
95720 to 95779		60	Rebuilt by GN with 20 inch extensions

Note: The above sets of cars are close to or exceptionally close to the Walthers HO model. Check photographs for rivet placements, etc. for other details.

Also refer to THE GREAT NORTHERN 75-TON ORE CAR FLEET, Reference Sheet No. 278, December, 1999, by the Great Northern Railway Historical Society.

Number Series	Built	Qty	Remarks
87000 to 97249	1924	250	Tapered Side, Built by Bethlehem Steel
87250 to 87999	1923	750	Tapered Side, Built by Bethlehem Steel
88000 to 88499	1920	500	Tapered Side, Built by AC&F
88500 to 88999	1920	500	Tapered and Slope Ends, Built by H&B

The tail end of this all-rail train at Northtown (the former Northern Pacific Twin Cities yard) includes a group of six box car red BN hoppers trailing a string of B&LE ore cars. When this photograph was taken, the caboose no longer graced the rear-end of the all-rail ore trains.
PATRICK C. DORIN

The next group of cars was delivered by Johnstown-America in 1992. Car 98039 (series 98000-98099) was part of the second-last group ordered by Burlington Northern. Again we have a different lettering arrangements on the cars. ROBERT BLOMQUIST

Photographed in November 1998, car 98113 was part of the 98100-98189 series—built in 1995 by Johnstown-America, the smallest order placed by the BN since 1976. This was the last group of cars to be painted with BN reporting marks. A new era was right around the corner. ROBERT BLOMQUIST

Still another group of 90 ore cars was ordered by the newly merged company, Burlington Northern Santa Fe. This new car, No. 601146 (601090-601179) was built by Johnstown-America in 1996. The group was equipped with an electric brake system. The BNSF insignia was placed on a steel plate on the upper-right corner of the car. However, they caused a bit of a problem by falling off from time to time. ROBERT BLOMQUIST

basic designs and carried BN or BNSF reporting marks. The accompanying photos and equipment rosters provide a look at the BN/BNSF ore car equipment.

TONNAGE AND TRENDS

The ore-hauling history of the GN/NP/BN/BNSF now extends for more than 110 years. The first boat was loaded in November 1892 on the Duluth & Winnipeg Railroad's first ore dock in Allouez.

Although train traffic is far less, excitement continues between Superior and the Mesabi Range via the Duluth & Winnipeg, Great Northern, Burlington Northern, and the Burlington Northern Santa Fe.

BNSF in 2002 served but two plants with the following potential annual production:

HibTac	8.4 Million Tons
National	5.3 Million Tons

The grand total of 13.7 million tons is just a little over one-third of the record tonnages moved over the former Great Northern in 1953, when 36 million tons of all types of ore was shipped.

BNSF ORE TRAIN SYMBOLS

Note: The "XX" after a train symbol indicates the number of trains operated thus far for the year. For example, "70" would mean the 70th train operated.

Dock Train Symbols:

Allouez–Hibbing Taconite
U ALLBRMOXX   Empties to HibTac
U BRMALLOXX   Loads to Allouez

Allouez–Keewatin
U ALLKEEOXX   Empties to Keewatin
U KEEALLOXX   Loads to Allouez

BNSF received 220 cars from Johnstown-America in 1998. No. 601228 (601180-601399) carries the latest lettering scheme as of the year 2001.

BNSF rebuilt over 200 cars in 1998 with covers for a special iron ore traffic in the south that never materialized. These 1998 views of Nos. 600012 and the 600171 illustrate both sides of the rebuilt cars. They were rebuilt from cars built in 1976.

The cars returned to Superior, Wisconsin, for regular ore service without the covers. No. 600000 was the first car in the series 600000-600374. Note the end extension at both ends of the car. The were added to eliminate spillage over the ends of the cars. ALL, ROBERT BLOMQUIST

It is May 1981, and freshly painted BN ore cars are about to be moved from the 28th Street Yard—Superior to Allouez. Since the train must be pushed from Saunders to Allouez, the caboose will be the lead car with the yard foreman providing information to the engineer for a safe movement. ROBERT BLOMQUIST

In November 1998 BNSF SD9 No. 6108, in a color scheme that creates memories of the Great Northern, is shoving a cut of ore cars with covers to the Allouez Yard. The train is en route from the Superior 28th Street Yard to the ore yard via Saunders. ROBERT BLOMQUIST

All-Rail Symbols:

Keewatin–Madison, Illinois (Granite City)
J MADALLOXX   Empties to Allouez
J ALLKETOXX   Allouez–Keewatin empties
J KEEMADOXX   Keewatin–Granite City loads

Saunders–Birmingham, Alabama
(Interchanged with DM&IR at Saunders)
J SAUBIROXX   Minntac loads to B'ham
JBIRSAUOXX   Empties to Minntac

Allouez–Madison
J ALLMADOXX   Loads to Granite City when loaded at Allouez

ABOVE: What about some of the other train operations on the BN/BNSF ore lines? This July 4, 1977, photo illustrates an ore transfer run at Calumet, Minnesota, meeting a loaded ore train en route to Superior powered by General Electric units. The transfer is performing both local freight work as well as serving mines. The caboose is an ex-Great Northern wooden car. Note the train order signal in front of the depot. It is in the yellow position, indicating train orders for the ore train. The pick-up hoops are next to the track and the engineer already has his arm out to pick up the orders for the head end. The lower hoop, barely visible, contains the orders for the conductor in the caboose. The train orders will provide authorization and instructions for running from Gunn eastward to Boylston.
ROBERT C. ANDERSON

3 NORTHSHORE MINING

ABOVE: The Northshore Mining Company ore car fleet consists of the former Reserve Mining Company Railroad's equipment. Many of the cars, like these photographed in August 1995, bore the "RM" reporting marks of their former owner. PATRICK C. DORIN

FACING PAGE: On September 14, 1997, Northshore Mining No. 1232 led a loaded train toward Silver Bay, Minnesota, near milepost 6. In a few minutes, the train will arrive at the dumping area for the Silver Bay plant. DAVID C. SCHAUER

Reserve Mining Company began operations in 1956 with an open-pit mine near Babbitt, Minnesota, and a pelletizing plant on Lake Superior at Silver Bay. The company constructed a single-track railroad for the 47-mile haul from the mine to the plant. During the first year of operation, 3.75 million tons of pellets were produced. The total jumped to 5 million tons in 1957.

In order to produce five million tons of pellets, the Reserve Mining Company Railroad handled 15 million tons of raw taconite ore from the mine to the plant. The ore was handled in 30-foot-long, flat-bottom, rotary dump ore cars—the only such equipment ever operated in the Lake Superior region.

Reserve Mining Company expanded the production capacity of the Silver Bay plant to ten million tons annually in 1960.

ESERVE MINING/ YPRESS NORTH SHORE

Where does it all begin for Northshore Mining? The mine at Babbit produces the raw taconite ore for the longest haul from mine to plant on the Mesabi Range.
BASGEN PHOTOGRAPHY,
DAN MACKEY COLLECTION

The loading facility at Babbitt is the final step in the mining process as the cars are loaded and prepared for the trip to the Silver Bay plant.
BASGEN PHOTOGRAPHY,
DAN MACKEY COLLECTION

At the same time, the 47-mile railroad was double-tracked. In order to produce ten million tons, the railroad handled nearly 31 million tons of taconite ore. This placed the railroad among the top three ore haulers in the country with the DM&IR and Great Northern.

The railroad climbs from 867 feet above sea level in Silver Bay to 1794 feet by milepost 18, then drops 188 feet to Babbitt. The maximum grade for the eastbound trains is 0.5 percent while the westbound is 1.5 percent.

Reserve Mining Company continued operating through the 1980s. In early 1980, the company established a new dumping ground for tailings about seven miles from the Silver Bay plant and away from Lake Superior. This added a new train operation with about four dump car trains per day hauling the tailings to the dump area. However, business was slipping for a variety of reasons.

Reserve's pellet production in 1975 was close to seven million tons. This slipped to six million in 1980 with a further drop to just over three million tons in 1985. This meant that the railroad was handling about nine million tons of raw ore for the production of three million tons. The company went into bankruptcy in 1986 and discontinued all operations.

A new company by the name of Cyprus North Shore was created in January 1990. Exten-

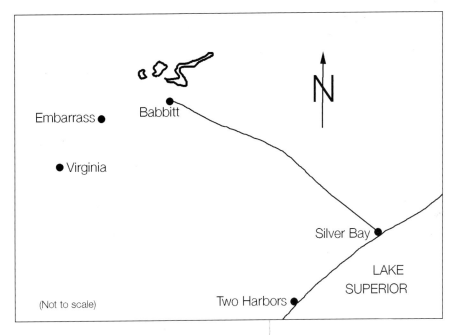

sive rebuilding was done at the Silver Bay plant and pellet production began to grow. Another name change came about in 1994 when Cyprus was purchased by Cleveland Cliffs Inc. The new name was Northshore Mining Company. Annual production was running close to about four million tons throughout the late 1990s, which in turn meant about 12 million tons of taconite ore was being hauled annually over the Northshore Mining Company Railroad.

A Northshore Mining empty train powered by four units rolls past milepost 23 on August 29, 1998.
DAVID C. SCHAUER

Northshore Mining's newest power, three SD40-3s, lead 156 loaded ore cars out of the Babbitt loading yard on June 15, 2001. PATRICK C. DORIN

The company in early 2002 was operating two to three 156-car trains per day for ore, and another three to four tailings trains per day. When business is at higher levels, train traffic ranges from 4 to 5 trains per day. Part of the main line is double-tracked and is equipped with Centralized Traffic Control (CTC).

The Northshore ore train crews originate at Babbitt and run a turn to the Silver Bay plant. The loaded trains are yarded at the plant, and the crew picks up an empty train to return to the mine.

A switch crew spots the loaded cars at the plant dumper on top of the hill above the plant. The entire dumping cycle for a train, two cars at a time including spotting the cars automatically, rolling over and return, takes about 90 minutes.

continued on page 76

Four units—1230, 1227, 1233 and 1229—lead a loaded train toward Silver Bay near milepost 6 in August 1995. The four-unit combination includes three SD18R's plus a single SD28, No. 1233. The flat-bottom ore cars are perfect for handling the raw taconite ore from Babbitt to the Silver Bay plant. The 150-car train slows as it rolls around the curve. Northshore Mining has been operating, on the average, three loaded trains per day.
PATRICK C. DORIN

A loaded train led by SD18R No. 1230 approaches the Silver Bay facility on May 25, 1997.
DAVID C. SCHAUER

Tailings trains operate from Silver Bay to the Dumping Ground near milepost 6. Some tailings trains travel all the way to the mine at Babbitt. Crushed tailings are used for the mine roads. This train has emptied its loaded cars and is about to depart for Silver Bay.

Tailings trains consist of dump cars and a caboose for the remote control operations.

The loaded train's caboose and compressor car were on the rear end for their westbound movement from Silver Bay to Babbitt. For the empty return trip, the motive power simply runs around the train.
ALL, PATRICK C. DORIN

Another view of a tailings train, near milepost 5 on September 14, 1997. Power is provided by three SD28s in the former Reserve Mining Company color scheme. DAVID C. SCHAUER

Caboose No. 20 brings up the rear of the tailings train at milepost 5 on this pleasant fall day in September, 1997. DAVID C. SCHAUER

An aerial view of the Silver Bay arrival yard, with the dumping facility to the left and the pelletizing plant and ore dock system visible at the right. BASGEN PHOTOGRAPHY, DAN MACKEY COLLECTION

OVERLEAF: The Silver Bay plant, with the ore loading dock and the *Thomas R. Patton* in the foreground. Note the train on the top of the hill, as well as the city of Silver Bay, Minnesota. BASGEN PHOTOGRAPHY, DAN MACKEY COLLECTION

The newest ore cars are painted black with white lettering and a yellow panel at one end of the car. The cars are being relettered NSMX as shown here with car 1157 in August 1998. PATRICK C. DORIN

In some cases, there are a few cars with the light coloring and the words "Reserve Mining." No. 370, photographed in August 1995, had its "RM" reporting marks and number located on the panel before the grab irons to the left side of the car. PATRICK C. DORIN

Cars 1168 and 1165 illustrate the application of the yellow striping. PATRICK C. DORIN

Northshore Mining owns a fleet of ballast cars that resemble tapered-side ore cars with extensions. Cars are painted black with orange center sections, and numbered in the 1400 series. PATRICK C. DORIN

The Reserve/Northshore operation is the opposite of all the other operations in the Lake Superior region. All other plants are located on the respective ranges with the pellets being shipped to the lake port. Northshore handles the raw ore to the plant and the pellets are loaded directly into boats at an adjacent storage and dock area.

With the reopening of the plant and mine in 1990, there has been a sense of optimism within the communities of Babbitt and Silver Bay. It is good to see something turn around in a positive direction. The new Northshore color scheme of blue and white reflects a bright direction in iron ore railroading on Lake Superior's North Shore.

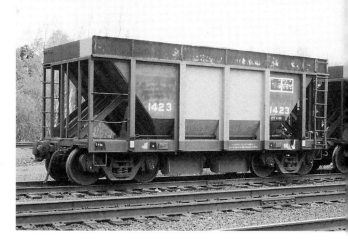

THE ORE CAR FLEET

The original ore car fleet for Reserve consisted of 090 cars in 1956. As of 2002, the Northshore fleet consisted of 635 cars numbered from 100 to 1104. The company purchased a fleet of new cars numbered 1150 to 1191, which are painted black with a yellow stripe and lettered NSMX.

The tail end of an ore train heads east toward Silver Bay at milepost 6 on June 15, 2001. PATRICK C. DORIN

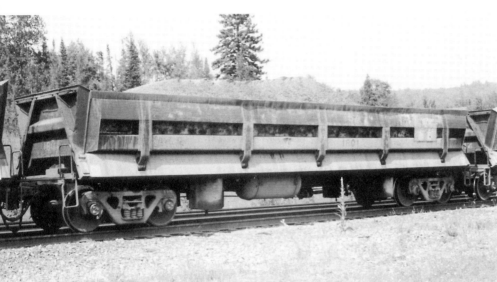

Tailings service is provided with dump cars like Nos. 1801 and 1905, both photographed in August 1995. BOTH, PATRICK C. DORIN

MOTIVE POWER

Reserve Mining Company

Type	Number Series	Built
SW8	1200 and 1201	1952
SW9	1211	1953
SW1200	1212	1962
SD9	1220-1225	1955-59
SD18	1226-1232	1960-62
SD28	1233-1236	1965

Northshore Mining (Mid-1990s)

Type	Number Series	Built
SW9	1211	1953
SW1200	1212	1962
GP9	1215	1956
SD9	1225	1959
SD18R	1226-1232	1991
SD28	1233-1236	1991

Northshore Mining Motive Power (June 2001)

Type	Number Series	Operation
SW1000	1212	Remote
SW1200	1214	Remote
SD18	1226, 1231	Remote
SD18	1230, 1232	
SD28	1234, 1235	Remote
SD28	1236	
SD40-3	650-652	
SD40-3	653, 654	Remote (Distributed Power)

SD18R No. 1231, shown in 1998, is equipped for remote control operation for tailings train service.

The Northshore Mining color scheme is blue with white trim and lettering. An insignia is located to the rear of the cab with the name "Northshore Mining" at the rear of the unit as on SD28 No. 1233.

SD18R No. 1228 still carried the Reserve Mining Company brown colors in 1995. Although difficult to see, the words Reserve Mining were painted over to the rear of the long hood. ALL, PATRICK C. DORIN

Northshore Mining SD28 No. 1234 still carried the remains of the Reserve Mining Company color scheme—a basic reddish brown—in 1998. PATRICK C. DORIN

The newest locomotives in Northshore service as of 2001 were the SD40-3s. No. 651 illustrates the lettering application on the left side. PATRICK C. DORIN

No. 652 illustrates the right side of the SD40-3 fleet. PATRICK C. DORIN

ERIE MINING CO./ LTV STEEL

ABOVE: An LTV ore train blasts out of the Cramer Tunnel in September 1995 with a string of classic F9s leading the show. DAVID C. SCHAUER

FACING PAGE: A view of the spectacular Taconite Harbor dock during the dumping process for a train on July 5, 1998. DAVID C. SCHAUER

Rail enthusiasts rallied for a final look at the LTV Steel Railroad, formerly the Erie Mining Company Railroad, in 2001. One of the major reasons was the fleet of F9s that were still powering the ore trains between Hoyt Lakes and Taconite Harbor in the Minnesota Arrowhead Country. The classic motive power continued to make history in the production and transportation of taconite pellets in the Lake Superior region.

The history of the Erie Mining Company can be traced back to 1931 when Pickands Mather, in conjunction with Bethlehem Steel Company and Youngstown Sheet & Tube, began research on processing low-grade iron ores. The Erie Mining Company was formed in 1940 after research and exploration demonstrated the extent of ore reserves and the potential for the successful

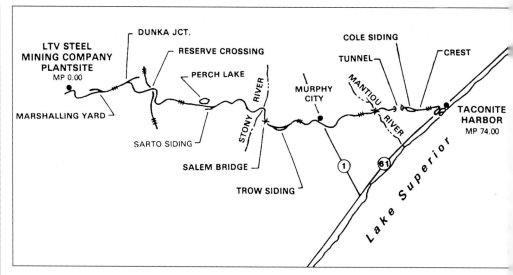

The LTV Railroad line extends from the taconite plant near Hoyt Lakes to Taconite Harbor on Lake Superior. LTV

Northern Minnesota is a spectacular area to photograph train operations. An LTV Steel Mining Company ore train with an F9 leading (No. 4211) and three leased units following is rolling toward Taconite Harbor on July 4, 1998. Train 4211 East is near the Cramer Tunnel, approximately 62.4 miles east of Knox. DAVID C. SCHAUER

processing of taconite ore into high grade pellets. A test and research pelletizing plant was built by the Erie Mining Company in 1948 and provided the ground work and knowledge necessary for the construction of the large-scale plant at Hoyt Lakes beginning in 1954. Three years later, in September 1957, production began with a 73.84 mile railroad to between Hoyt Lakes and Taconite Harbor including the return loop at the new ore dock.

Taconite Harbor is approximately 72 miles northeast of Duluth at a location known as Two Islands. August Maebius, an engineer for Great Lakes Dock & Dredge Company from the 1930s through the 1950s, reported to this writer that a railroad line and ore dock system had been proposed early in the 20th century for the Two Islands harbor. There was mixed speculation that the Duluth & Iron Range Railway, or a new railroad, would be the builder.

A six-unit "covered wagon" combination on the head-end of an LTV ore train, with F9 4210 in the lead. The train is near the Trow siding. DAVID C. SCHAUER

The operations of the Erie Mining Company, renamed LTV Steel Mining Company when purchased by LTV Steel in 1986, had not changed dramatically since operations began in 1957. The railroad celebrated its 40th year of operation in 1997.

MINE RUN OPERATIONS

The Erie/LTV mine run operations consisted of side-dump cars powered by one or two diesel units depending upon the type of work handled by a particular assignment. The side-dump cars were built by Magor and Difco between 1957 and 1971. All of the mine run trains were handled by locomotives equipped with radio-remote control. Each train was handled by one person who operated the train from the mine loading pockets to the plant crusher.

There were two sets of routes serving the raw ore mines for the pelletizing plant. The primary mines were located near the plant. There were nine different pits, up to six of which were used at any one time. The dump-car trains had short runs (from 1.5 to six miles) from the mines to the crusher. Trains consisted of either nine or 18 cars with one or two units, respectively.

The other mine was the Dunka Mine, located on a branch line that left the main line about 9.8 miles east of Knox. The Dunka Mine was served by 36-car trains which operated between the mine and the plant. The company assigned an Alco C-424 to the Dunka Mine operation until it was closed in 1994.

The mine run trains included a control-cab-equipped dump-car on the rear of the train. The individual crew member would ride in this compartment when the train was operating in the reverse direction. One could call it a "push-pull" operation, similar in this regard to some commuter train services.

LTV Steel operated Baldwin S-12 switch engines for train assembly and part of the mine run operations. Here, No. 7245 is handling a group of cars at Knox for assembly into a road train for Taconite Harbor. Knox is the western end of the LTV Railroad, the former Erie Mining Company Railroad. PATRICK C. DORIN

An LTV ore train is going through the process of unloading taconite pellets as it moves across the Taconite Harbor ore dock on July 4, 1998. As soon as the train is empty, it will continue around the looping track arrangement and return to Knox and the taconite plant. DAVID C. SCHAUER

The LTV mine runs provided a crucial part in the movement of the ore from the mine to the plant. Once the ore was crushed and processed into the taconite pellets, it was ready for stockpiling and eventual loading into a road train for transfer to the ore dock at Taconite Harbor.

THE MAIN LINE TO TACONITE HARBOR

The Erie Mining/LTV road trains were something to see. During the 1990s, and even into the year 2001, the trains were powered by Electro-Motive F9s, sometimes in four- or five-unit combinations. This changed with the loss of part of the F9 fleet because of a major derailment in January 1997. Road power in the final years included the F9s with GP20s, GP38s, and sometimes leased units.

The pellet cars were loaded at the plant and then switched into a complete train. When the appropriate number of cars had been loaded for a train, i.e., 96 or 120 cars, a crew was called.

The crew reported to the Knox Yard Office ju to the east of the pelletizing plant, picked u their motive power and backed to the yard track with the loaded cars. The train was then assem bled by the road crew and once the air brake tes had been completed, the loaded train departe for Taconite Harbor. It took approximately thre hours for the one-way trip through the beautifu northern Minnesota wilderness.

This wilderness area is very remote and cor sequently crews had an opportunity to see a var ety of wildlife. This included moose who are no always thrilled when a train is moving throug their territory. Most of the time, the moose wise ly decided to leave the LTV train alone and sim ply ran into the woods—but not always.

As the loaded trains departed Knox Yarc they climbed steadily to the summit (milepo. 44.0) just east of Trow. From Trow to the Ha bor, the trains had a descending grade. A passin siding is located both at Trow and Tunnel wit shorter sidings at Reserve, Sarto, and Murph Tunnel is located just outside of the tunnel a milepost 62.4

The track to Dunka was also used as a single-ended passing siding. Tunnel was originally named Cole, but the name was changed shortly after going to operation because the name Cole sounded too much like Trow on the radio.

Upon arrival at the Harbor, the train moved out on to the ore dock and unloaded the pellets while in motion. This unloading operation was one of the most unique systems to be found anywhere in the world.

The pellet cars were equipped with an automobile tire on each side. One wheel was used to open the hopper doors, while the one the opposite side was used to close the doors. The wheels contacted a rail and as the car moved forward the wheels (tires) rotated to either open or close the doors. The pellet dock rail was mounted in an upside down position on 76 moveable pedestals beside each of the 25 dock bins. It was raised into position when desired to contact the tires to open the hopper doors. As the car emptied and rose on its springs, the tire was lifted clear of the dumping rail. A rail on the opposite side of the track past the last dock bin contacted all tires to close the doors as the train began to make its move around the loop. Once the train was unloaded, which took anywhere from seven to 15 minutes, it began its trip back to Hoyt Lakes. An entire round trip could take from seven to eight hours.

The LTV road operations were the opposite of many other rail lines in the Lake Superior region. With most train operations, the road crews are called from the lake port and run to the mines and return. LTV crews operated from the range to the port and return.

Although the pellet trains operated only during the shipping season from as early as mid-March to as late as mid-January, trains did operate over the main line throughout the entire year. An ash train operated from the Taconite Harbor power plant to the Hoyt Lakes plant site where the ash was disposed of as landfill. This train operated about twice a week. This operation lasted about three years, ending in July 2000.

Erie Mining discontinued the use of cabooses in 1983, but the company retained one of the extended-vision cupola cabooses for work train service.

The Erie Mining/LTV road operations were exceptionally smooth. At its peak in the 1960s the line saw four to six loaded trains per day, meaning eight to twelve trains every 24-hour period. The 1980s and 1990s saw three to five loaded trains per day. Most of the meets were made at Trow.

It was a very effective and efficient operation, and when one considers the type of motive power in use, the F9s, it is not only historic but all the more impressive. It just goes to show what can be done with motive power taken care of properly ... however that is another story. Suffice to say, the Erie Mining/LTV trains were an impressive show.

THE TACONITE HARBOR ORE DOCK SYSTEM

The Erie Mining/LTV ore dock was actually the fastest train unloading facility on the Great Lakes. With the rubber-tire system, the company achieved a high car utilization seldom found elsewhere. Some of the ore cars could actually make two round trips within 24 hours with this unloading system.

The ore dock at Taconite Harbor has a total length of 2334 feet. The pellet storage area and boat loading facilities are 1200 feet long with a storage capacity of 100,000 tons. At the east end of the ore dock is a 510-foot-long coal dock for the power plant.

This aerial views shows the entire Taconite Harbor ore dock facility of the Erie Mining Company including the loop trackage (see track diagram on page 88). The trackage crossed highway 61, the North Shore highway between Duluth and Thunder Bay, three times.
BASGEN PHOTOGRAPHY,
DAN MACKEY COLLECTION

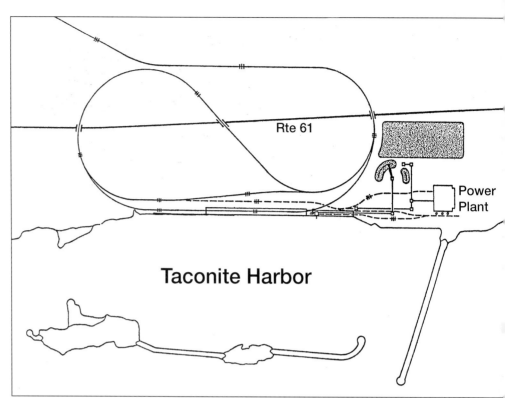

Trackage diagram of the Taconite Harbor facility. LTV

Close-up view of the loading chutes in action at the Taconite Harbor ore dock. BASGEN PHOTOGRAPHY, DAN MACKEY COLLECTION

The ore dock contains 25 pellet storage bins on 48-foot centers, each of which is serviced by a retractable conveyor belt system to load the pellets into the ore boats. The conveyors are 42 inches wide and have a total shuttle length of 91 feet. Their maximum reach beyond the ore dock face is 44 feet, with a height of 37 feet above the water. The belts can move at speeds of 250 to 500 feet per minute, which means that each belt can load in excess of 1500 tons per hour—18,000 tons of pellets can be loaded into a boat in about four or five hours.

Taconite Harbor, having been built in 1957, is still one of the newest dock systems for ore handling on the Great Lakes. Its last year of operation for loading ships was 2001.

THE MOTIVE POWER FLEET

The Erie and LTV Steel Mining Company motive power roster comprised locomotives from EMD, Alco, and Baldwin.

LTV No.	Type	Former Erie Mining No.
4201 - 4204	GP38-3	1997 - 98
4206 - 4209	GP20-M	1994 - 95
4210 - 4214	F9	100 - 104
4215 - 4216	GP38	7250 - 7251, 700 - 701
4220 - 4225	F9B	200 - 205
7200 - 7214	RS-11	300 - 314
7215 - 7216	RS-11	
7220 - 7222	C-420	350 - 352, 600 - 602
7230	C-424	500
7240 - 7248	S-12	400 - 408

Motive power off the roster at railroad shutdown: 4212, 4213, 4220, 4221, 7200, 7203, 7240 - 7244, 7246.

THE PELLET CAR FLEET

The Erie Mining/LTV ore car fleet was built in 1956, with additional cars constructed in 1997 to replace equipment lost in the major derailment. There were originally 389 cars with a lightweight of 60,400 pounds each. The capacity of these cars was 190,600 pounds or 95 tons. The coupled length is 37' 8". They were equipped with roller bearings, automatic empty and load brakes, single-clasp-type composition brake shoes, and 36-inch multiple-wear wheels.

Roster of LTV Equipment

Pellet Cars:
3000 to 3388
Note: Erie Mining Company original numbers.

Replacement Cars 3401 to 3496

Crude Ore Car Fleet
Magor   1601 to 1810, Built 1956
Difco   1811 to 1930, Built 1965
Note: Difco also supplied cab cars about 1971.

In September 1995, a special passenger train for a mining engineers' group operated from Knox to Taconite Harbor and return. F-units led a mixture of passenger equipment from the Lake Superior Railroad Museum. The train is returning to Knox in this late afternoon photo. PATRICK C. DORIN

In this 1995 view, F9B 4222 shows how the color scheme continued including the yellow ends. The B-units played a major role in the LTV roster through the late 1990s. PATRICK C. DORIN

LTV owned four GP20-M's, such as the 4206 and 4209. The two units as well as the 4208 were resting between assignments when photographed at Knox in 1995. PATRICK C. DORIN

GP38 No. 4216 was one of two such units owned by LTV. No. 4216 still carried its Erie Mining Company lettering when photographed at Knox in 1995. PATRICK C. DORIN

SHUTDOWN

In its 40-plus years of service, the Erie/LTV operation was a testimonial to how successful a railroad can be as the link between natural resources and manufactured products. It is indeed a sa note that LTV suspended the mining operatio in early 2001, leaving only the stockpiles to handled to Taconite Harbor before the railro was shut down that summer.

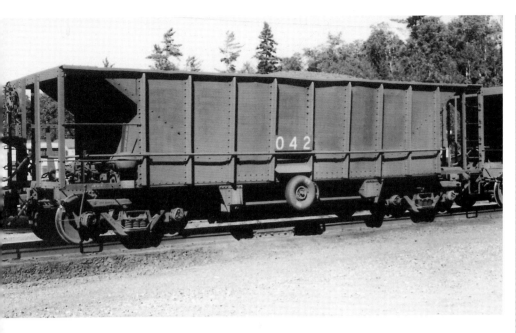

LTV operated a fleet of pellet cars such as Nos. 42 and 266 illustrated here in mid-1995. The cars were once lettered for the Erie Mining Company, with EMTX reporting marks. The capacity was 90 to 95 tons. PATRICK C. DORIN

In 1997 LTV ordered some additional ore cars of 100-ton capacity. These cars carried the reporting marks LTVX. No. 3409 was photographed at the DM&IR's interchange yard adjacent to the ore docks in Duluth. STEVEN RUCE

5 SOO LINE

ABOVE: Soo Line rectangular-side Minnesota ore car 91956 is very similar to the Walthers HO-scale model—the exceptions are the name plate and the welded sides rather than the rivets. This type of equipment never saw service on the Michigan ore lines. JIM MORIN

FACING PAGE: Soo No. 798 and DM&IR No. 116 roll by the Nemadji station sign as they lead an empty ore train bound from Superior to the Cuyuna Range on August 3, 1978. TOM CARLSON

The Cuyuna Range was the largest of the Soo Line's ore operations. It extended from Superior to Ironton, Minnesota, a distance of over 100 miles. In fact, the ore routing was the longest ore line in the United States. Only the Canadian National had longer distances for its ore traffic.

What made the Soo Line unique was its ore pooling operation with the Northern Pacific. Under this arrangement, established in 1928, the two companies split ore traffic and revenues on a 50/50 basis. In 1970, however, the Northern Pacific became a key part of newly created Burlington Northern and things changed immediately.

The Northern Pacific ore dock was closed and all Soo Line ore trains began operating to the former Great Northern Allouez Ore Yard. This operation continued

Soo 798 and DM&IR 116 roll their train of empty ore cars past the depot at Moose Lake on August 3, 1978. Tom Carlson

The Soo's Minnesota ore lines extended from Superior to Moose Lake and beyond to Ironton, Minnesota. The Soo Line had trackage rights over the Northern Pacific line west of McGregor. All-rail ore routes for the Soo Line extended from Superior to Chicago as well as Minneapolis to Chicago. Some Great Northern all-rail ore trains were interchanged with the Soo Line in Minneapolis. Soo Line

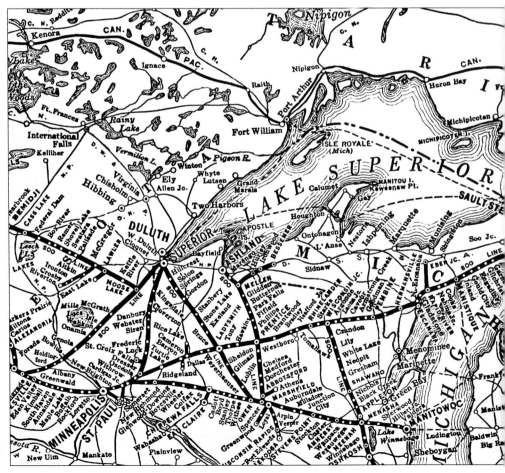

SOO LINE "MINNESOTA" ORE CAR ROSTER SUMMARY

70-Ton Capacity
Number Series

81850 to 82049
   Rectangular-side cars built by the Soo Line in 1950 with welded sides plus a name plate.

81600 to 81724
   Tapered-side cars with Minnesota dimensions and specifications. Built by Pullman in 1925.

81725 to 81849
   Tapered-side cars built by American Car & Foundry in 1925.

The following 50-ton ore cars were operated by the Soo Line on the Cuyuna and Michigan ranges

80000 to 80100
   Summers ore car built by Standard Steel Car in 1910.

80508 to 80807
   Sloped-end cars built by American Car & Foundry in 1913.

81300 to 81599
   Sloped-end cars built by Haskell and Barker in 1920.

80200 to 80499
   Rectangular-side car with ribs (see page 172 of *Soo Line*, Superior Publishing Company, 1979).

In July 1981, Soo Line No. 4428 leads sisters 4412 and 4425 as a loaded ore train prepares to depart the New Yard at Ironton, Minnesota, bound for Superior, Wisconsin. The train consists of DM&IR ore cars. TOM CARLSON

until about 1980, when the Allouez facility began handling only taconite pellets. Soo Line ore trains were then interchanged with the Duluth, Missabe & Iron Range Railway in Superior, and the ore was shipped from the DM&IR docks in Duluth. This lasted a short time, and the last Soo Line ore train ran in the fall of 1984.

The final years of operations saw only Soo Line activity on the Cuyuna Range. Burlington Northern, more or less, gave it up. The annual tonnages were incredibly small, i.e., less than 100,000 tons per year. There were no longer any mine run operations. The Soo Line road crews would deliver the empty ore cars, tie up for an eight-hour rest, go back to work, switch the loads into the train, and return to Superior. The Virginia Mine was the last ore producer on the Cuyuna Range.

The Soo operated its own Minnesota-type ore cars, mixed in with 50-ton-capacity ore cars. During the last months of operation, the Soo ore cars were replaced with DM&IR equipment. None of the Soo Line cars received any side extensions for pellet service.

Some of the ore cars later went into rock and ballast service but were scrapped as time went on. All of the cars were off the roster by the late 1980s, prior to the inclusion of the Soo Line into the Canadian Pacific Railway System. Wouldn't it have been interesting to see Soo ore cars repainted with the words, "Canadian Pacific" with SOO reporting marks!

Soo Line ore Extra 4425 East departs Ironton on July 28, 1981. Caboose 129 brings up the rear as the loads move out to Superior over Burlington Northern trackage rights—formerly Northern Pacific. TOM CARLSON

ABOVE LEFT: This Soo Line ore train represents the type of trains operated in the Soo-Northern Pacific ore pool since the 1930s—with the exception of steam power, of course. The trains were a mixture of Soo and NP ore cars and were powered by EMD GP7s, GP9s, GP30s, and GP35s on the Soo from the 1950s through the early 1980s. A mixture of GP9s and Alco road switchers operated on the NP from the 1950s through the BN merger in 1970. PATRICK C. DORIN

ABOVE RIGHT: Not only did the Soo Line lease DM&IR ore cars for service on the Cuyuna Range, but the company also borrowed motive power. In this case, it is late in the evening near Saunders (south side of Superior) during the summer of 1978 as DM&IR No. 130 approaches the interlocking limits with two Soo GP9s and 200 loaded cars of ore. PATRICK C. DORIN

6   CANADIAN NATIONAL

ABOVE: Extra CN 5582 East is at milepost 58.4 of the Kashabowie Subdivision on August 3, 1978, with a train consisting of loaded ore cars from Steep Rock and Caland mines as well as some general freight bound for Thunder Bay.
BRYAN E. MARTYNIUK

FACING PAGE: This top-side view of the Canadian National ore dock in Thunder Bay, Ontario, shows the pockets for unloading. The CNR's lone Fairbanks-Morse (CLC) 2400-horsepower Train Master, No. 2900, has just completed a shove to the dock and is carefully spotting cars over the appropriate pockets for a specific shipping order.
CANADIAN NATIONAL

The CNR was a relative newcomer to the Lake Superior iron ore railroads club, and of course, along with the Soo Line and others, it is out of that business.

The CNR's first ore operations began in Atikokan, Ontario, in 1944 with the traffic moving "west" to Fort Frances, and then south over subsidiary Duluth, Winnipeg & Pacific Railway to Superior, Wisconsin. The first ore was shipped over the Great Northern docks until the CNR dock was built in Port Arthur, Ontario, in 1945. With the completion of the newest and last pocket-type ore dock on the Great Lakes, the ore moved from Atikokan to Port Arthur, a distance of 140 miles. Ore shipments over this segment of the railroad ended in 1980. The ore dock saw some coal traffic for a while, but the dock and yard were dismantled.

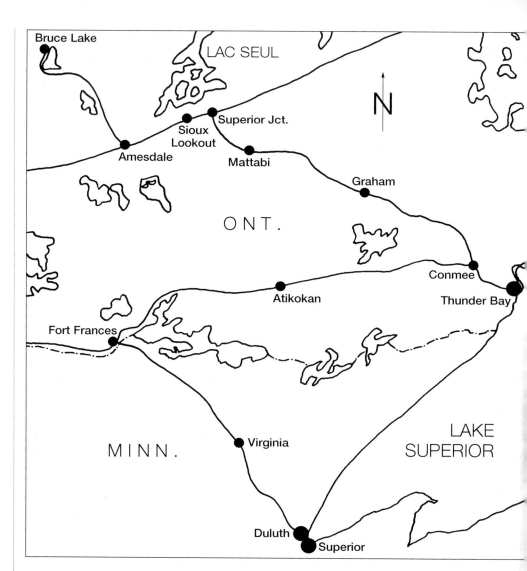

The Canadian National ore dock at Thunder Bay was a spectacular sight at night. The dock's lighting system gave off an aura of both peace and excitement with boat loadings and the ore switching moves to and from the dock. The *Edward L. Ryerson* was photographed in September 1960 while getting ready to take on a load of ore from Inland Steel's ore mine and plant near Atikokan, Ontario. INLAND STEEL COMPANY, PATRICK C. DORIN COLLECTION

Only the concrete structure remains standing—a very sad sight.

A second Canadian National iron ore operation commenced in 1968 with the start-up of a pelletizing plant at Bruce Lake, Ontario. This mine was located 253 miles northwest of Thunder Bay (see map on facing page). The pellets were shipped in conventional 24-foot ore cars and dumped at the remodeled Valley Camp Coal Company dock. This operation was discontinued in 1990, when the exciting chapter of Canadian National ore operations with 24-foot ore cars and the rich variety of CN motive power came to an end.

Although CN served mines in northwestern Ontario, these iron ore deposits were at least distantly related to the Mesabi, Vermilion, and Gunflint ranges in northeastern Minnesota.

Ore car No. 341127, at Thunder Bay, Ontario, in October 1985, is from the 62.5-ton capacity group, which was the first set of ore cars purchased by the CNR for the new Steep Rock services around 1944. The cars are virtually identical to the later 82.5-ton design, but were narrower (see dimensions in the roster). Note that the car has but two braces, instead of the four shown on the 341043 below. THOMAS A. DORIN

No. 341043 is another example of the small 62.5-ton capacity CN ore car, photographed in October 1985. Note, however, that this car has been equipped with four braces instead of the usual two found with this group. THOMAS A. DORIN

In October 1985, 82.5-ton No. 343076 retained its original lettering.

The CN ore cars were also rebuilt with 18-inch extensions such as No. 344604, shown in October 1985. BOTH, THOMAS DORIN

The 18-inch extension is shown on No. 344029 at Fort Rouge, Man., in July 1987. STAFFORD SWAIN

CN No. 343052 displays the final paint and lettering scheme on the company's ore car fleet. PAT DORIN

The Duluth, Winnipeg & Pacific purchased a fleet of ore cars from the DM&IR, which were converted to stone and/or rock ballast service. They were painted CN orange and kept the DM&IR high-level air hose connections. No. 53313 was at the DW&P's Pokegama Yard near Superior, Wisconsin. PATRICK C. DORIN

The tail end of a westbound empty ore train bound for the ore mines at Atikokan in mid-1977 has just departed Conmee at milepost 35.7 of Canadian National's Kashabowie Subdivision. The double track in the background is Canadian Pacific's main line (Kaministiquia Subdivision). Conmee was CN's junction point with the Graham Subdivision to Sioux Lookout. The bridge over the river marks the beginning of the Graham Subdivision.
BRYAN E. MARTYNIUK

Extra CN 5010 West is at milepost 1.5 on the Graham Subdivision with an empty ore train on January 7, 1986. The Graham Sub was used by trains to serve two ore mines. The Mattabi Mine was located 13.6 miles northeast of Mattabi at milepost 119.6 on the Graham Sub. (119.6 miles west of Conmee). The Mattabi Spur was built in 1971. The Bruce Lake mine was situated on the Bruce Lake Subdivision, built in 1968. Ore trains traveled from Thunder Bay to Conmee and then to Sioux Lookout. At Sioux Lookout, the trains headed west on the Reditt Sub. to Carroll Junction (50.5 miles west of Sioux Lookout). The mine site was 66.3 miles north of the junction or 16.1 miles north of Ear Falls. The Bruce Lake Sub. was abandoned in 1988 after the mine shut down. BRYAN E. MARTYNIUK

CANADIAN NATIONAL ORE CAR ROSTER SUMMARY

Number Series	Capacity	Year	Remarks
114100 to 114699	62.5 tons	1944	Built by National Steel Car

Note: Although the cars are very similar to the Walthers HO-scale ore car, the 62.5 ton capacity cars are 9 feet, 7 inches wide instead of the usual 10 feet, 8 inches (plus or minus) for the "Minnesota" ore car group.

This group was renumbered as follows: 341000 to 341541 without extensions
                                        342117 to 342139 with extensions.

Number Series	Capacity	Year	Remarks
122000 to 123079	82.5 tons	1957	Built by National Steel Car

This group was renumbered as follows: 343000 to 343085 without extensions
                                        344000 to 344866 with extensions